In Sickness
and in Health

*Turning tragedy
into holiness*

Mary Flynn

BALBOA.
PRESS
A DIVISION OF HAY HOUSE

Balboa Press books may be ordered through booksellers or by contacting:

Balboa Press
A Division of Hay House
1663 Liberty Drive
Bloomington, IN 47403
www.balboapress.com
1 (877) 407-4847

Because of the dynamic nature of the Internet, any web addresses or links contained in this book may have changed since publication and may no longer be valid. The views expressed in this work are solely those of the author and do not necessarily reflect the views of the publisher, and the publisher hereby disclaims any responsibility for them.

The author of this book does not dispense medical advice or prescribe the use of any technique as a form of treatment for physical, emotional, or medical problems without the advice of a physician, either directly or indirectly. The intent of the author is only to offer information of a general nature to help you in your quest for emotional and spiritual well-being. In the event you use any of the information in this book for yourself, which is your constitutional right, the author and the publisher assume no responsibility for your actions.

Any people depicted in stock imagery provided by Thinkstock are models, and such images are being used for illustrative purposes only. Certain stock imagery © Thinkstock.

Print information available on the last page.

ISBN: 978-1-5043-8543-5 (sc)
ISBN: 978-1-5043-8544-2 (hc)
ISBN: 978-1-5043-8542-8 (e)

Library of Congress Control Number: 2017912097

Balboa Press rev. date: 12/01/2017

Dedicated to you.

A MOMENT CAN CHANGE YOUR LIFE forever. Sometimes one thing can happen that changes your life. In the spark of that moment you realize that life will never be the same. Whether you like it or not, life as you planned it, as you dreamed it, has changed... forever.

T HE CAB CAME TO AN abrupt, whiplash stop at the hospital's front entrance. In a whirlwind ride from the airport, dodging in and out of the heavy streams of New York traffic, missing the bike messengers by just a hair, we arrived at the hospital in Manhattan. I quickly opened the door while shoving money in the cab driver's hand not really caring how much I gave him. I just wanted out of the cab. I wanted to see my baby.

The hospital's sliding glass doors were dotted with greasy fingerprints. The moment I entered I was overwhelmed by the rancid smell of body odor. The waiting room was packed with people — young, old and many who looked like they had been sleeping on the streets for years. Some were sitting, others standing and quite a few were leaning on the walls, all waiting for their names to be called. "Johnson." I heard a nurse yell out into the waiting room. "Johnson. Is there anyone here named Johnson?" In the corner of the room, sat an old man looking through an outdated magazine. His stringy gray hair stuck out of his Yankees baseball cap, and his beard looked like it had food entangled in the strands. He slowly got up and shuffled toward the nurse. "Yea, I'm Johnson. It is about time. I have been sitting here for over five hours waiting for you to call my name." "Well, that I just did," said the nurse hurriedly directing him to the triage room. I glanced around the room trying to catch the eye of a staff member so that they could show me where my son was. But there was no one, except a police officer.

He was standing by a gray metal locked door that led to the ER treatment rooms. All dressed in his uniform with his right hand placed on his gun, he glanced around the room. I ran up to him and screamed, "Please let me in! My son is back there, and I need to see him now. Please I beg you, I need to see my baby!" He looked surprised as I ran toward him but he seemed to listen to what I was saying. He picked up the phone and dialed a number. "There is woman who says that her son is back there. Do you have a kid there?" And then he paused. "Okay. I will let her in."

He pulled out a ring of clanging keys from his pocket and unlocked the door. I ran down the narrow, dingy hallway. It was as if everything was in black and white, and I was running in slow motion. I couldn't get back there fast enough. Turning the corner of the hallway, I stopped dead in my tracks. It was all becoming so real. Stretchers were lined up and the curtains were open except for one: I knew my baby was behind that curtain. I ran past the doctor and nurses, stopped and then slowly pulled the curtain back. There he was, asleep on the stretcher, his face and arms were smudged with dirt, and his clothes looked ragged and old. He looked so tiny on such a long stretcher. Quietly walking to his side, careful not to wake him, I gently placed my hands under his limp body and pulled him close to my chest and deeply inhaled, taking in his smell, hearing the sound of his breath and feeling the weight of his little body in my arms.

Then I began to sing. It was the song I promised him that we would sing when I spoke to him on the phone in the ambulance — the song that we sang every night before he went to sleep. "Taste and see, taste and see." And with that he opened his swollen eyes and began to mouth the rest of the words, "...and see, taste and see." I stared into his blue eyes, afraid to close my eyes. I didn't want to take my eyes off him. How did he end up here, hundreds of miles away from home? How did my husband end up in jail? Why did this happen?

I WAS 33 YEARS OLD AND dated many men, but I never found the one. Don't get me wrong. There were a few diamonds in the rough ... very, very rough, but no one who captured my heart.

There was the guy who after I just met him said that he loved me. The next day he sent me the most beautiful flower arrangement (although they looked like they could have been on top of a casket). My colleagues at work asked me who my true love was, and I couldn't remember his name — not a good sign.

Then there was the guy who said I was "too intense" as we were driving in the car. I whipped my head toward him and insisted that he was not intense enough. That was the first and last date with him. And then, there was the really tall guy who said one smart thing the first time I met him ... and that was it. I even dated him for six months thinking that he would say something else intelligent. He didn't. After turning down his marriage proposal, I knew I was done ... with the dating scene and all the comedic suffering that went with it. It was time to focus my energy on something grander, something more exciting like a bucket list.

I had heard about a woman was left at the altar, so she wrote a bucket list of all the things that she ever wanted to do and then embarked on a quest to check them off, one by one. Since I wasn't going down the "normal" path of marriage and children, which in a way was a death itself, I decided it was time to write my own bucket list. I grabbed a notebook and pen and began jotting down all the things I wanted to do and see.

I had always wanted to go to Ireland and see where my ancestors lived. My parents named me after a great-aunt who lived in County Cork, so I had a close affinity to my Irish heritage (or maybe just the beer.) Anyway, I thought about herding sheep, hanging clothes on an outdoor line and sitting in an old Irish pub with the common folk, sipping a pint of their finest and listening to the man on a stool playing the mandolin to an old Irish tune. That sounded lovely.

And then I had thought about volunteering with a medical mission in Africa. Riding elephants to the remote village, setting up tents in the middle of nowhere, fighting off mosquitos at night and serving the medical needs of the people all seemed very appealing to me — except for the fact I am not a medical person, and I faint and throw up at the mere sight of blood. Ok, I scratched that one off my list.

And then of course, I wanted to be a lobster woman, working on a lobster boat in New England. I wanted to brave the wild seas, lowering the wooden traps into the water, and then bringing them back up crammed full with angry, claw-pinching lobsters. I tried once to get a job in that field. After graduate school I traveled up east for a week. With a resume in hand, I approached the dock where there were four gruff-looking unshaven men standing in a lobster boat preparing for their next voyage. I asked them if they were hiring and they looked at me and chuckled. They asked me if I had experience. I said, "not yet," and they said that they didn't have any openings. I am still bound and determined to check this one off my bucket list.

The remaining item on my list though was returning to England, where I lived for a few years when I was growing up. My father's company sent him over to start a new division so we went with him. There was something simply enchanting about the memories of that time of my life.

We moved to a small town outside of London when I was seven years old. I was born in Michigan and when my parents told my siblings and I that we were moving, I, for some odd reason thought we were moving to Illinois. We flew to New York and then boarded the enormous ship. For seven days, we sailed the turbulent waters of the Atlantic Ocean, and it was then that I had the inkling that Illinois was not our destination. After days of shivering on the deck of the ship and throwing up in the small, cramped cabin's bathroom, we docked in London and found ourselves in the midst of British accents, double-decker buses, black cabs, crown jewels and all else that seemed foreign to me. It definitely was not the farmland of Illinois.

My parents immediately signed my siblings and me up to attend an old, Catholic all girl's school. The campus was filled with old gray stone buildings, creaky oak wooden floors, muddy cricket fields and warm pints of milk that were stacked in rusty metal racks outside the double-glass doors of the main building. The mere smell of the sour milk nauseated me and made me gag on a daily basis. My mom finally wrote a note excusing me from drinking the milk. The nuns were reluctant at first but made the exception after seeing me throw up one too many times.

All the students looked alike because we all dressed alike — in boring evergreen uniforms, matching socks and brown buckled shoes. We carried our books in brown leather satchels that tugged heavily on our small shoulders, walked in straight lines, attended mass every day and said, "Yes, sister," to the nuns who were dressed in full habits. The hallways were long and narrow, and our footsteps echoed off the dirty brick walls leaving me with an eerie feeling and sending a cool chill down my spine. Hanging uneven on the wall were dusty portraits of nuns and priests who had worked at the school throughout the years. It was like looking at Leonardo da Vinci's "Mona Lisa." No matter where you walked, their eyes followed you. I think that was what Catholic guilt was all about.

I always believed that the school was haunted with spirits of ghosts and nuns from the past. My belief was so strong that when my mom would drop me off in the front of school in the wee hours of the morning, I would walk in the front door, sneak right out the back and run frantically all the way home. My mom and I would then get in the car and drive back to school. Sometimes we stopped at a local restaurant for hamburgers and strawberry shakes before returning to school. But my mood changed when we pulled up outside the massive front doors of the school. Shamefully, I walked into the classroom and apologized to Sister Mary Joseph, my teacher, for causing her unnecessary alarm. I don't think she even knew I was missing until I walked in that door with my mother.

Sister Mary Joseph wore a long black habit, masculine black shoes with ties laced up to the ankle and a veil that covered everything except her brown, beady eyes and pasty cheeks. She scared the living daylights out of me. I stood there, body trembling, "Sister Mary Joseph, I am sorry that I left school without telling anyone." Really, I wasn't sorry but I was afraid that if I didn't say that she would send me down to the hall to the Mother of all Mother's, the headmistress. And from what I heard from the other kids, that was a trip to hell, bypassing purgatory. So, I bit my tongue and just did it. "I am really, really sorry, Sister Mary Joseph. I won't do it again." With a quick nod of her head and the disapproving look from her eyes, she motioned me back to my desk in the back of the dimly lit classroom.

The embarrassment was over ... until the next day when the entire experience was repeated and I had to stand, shaking in my brown buckle shoes, apologizing once again to Sister Mary Joseph, begging for her unending forgiveness.

So I put England on the top of my bucket list but I needed to create a plan. After work, I would go to the local bookstore, sit on the carpeted floor with a cup of hot coffee by my side and rifle through every travel book they had on England. I jotted down the places I wanted to see again, like the small Catholic Church I received my first communion, and our beautiful old house with fireplaces in each room and a tennis court in our backyard. I became more excited as I planned the details of what I needed in order to make this adventure really happened. I needed a passport, plane reservations, hotel tickets and, oh, money. I needed money. So I started to pack away all of the money that was left over after paying the bills, which wasn't much. I opened a savings account at our local bank and kept depositing any dollar bills or change that I had.

With my list in hand, my life was beginning to feel full and surprisingly satisfying. At that time, I worked with a nonprofit agency that served the poor. We provided counseling, food, and clothing to those who lived in the inner city. I found myself mesmerized by my clients' often tragic but humble stories. Women would come into the office and sit for hours talking about their childhood and all that had happened to them. The women were poor economically but rich in spirit as they navigated through their difficult lives of poverty, violence and single parenting. My dad had always said there was no money working with the poor, and he was right but I truly loved it.

And then there was the soup kitchen. Once a week, I went down to the poor part of the city where a lot of homeless men and women slept on the streets and we served hot meals to them.

One man, Isaiah, was a regular. He looked like he was in his late 30s. He had long, black dreadlocks with white fuzz embedded in the woven braids, and it looked like he hadn't washed or combed his hair for years. He wore a long, bulky blue jacket with oversized pockets and holes the size of baseballs in the sleeves. His pants were dark blue, almost black as they looked as if they were once uniform pants for a mechanic at an auto repair shop. I could see his chafed, raw black skin through the holes in his coat, and his smell surrounded him like the cloud that followed Pigpen in the Peanuts comic strips.

His soft-spoken voice contradicted his rough exterior as he greeted me each day as if we were old friends. "Hey, Mary. How are your mom and dad doing?" "Fine, Isaiah. They are doing great. Thanks for asking." He nodded his head and mumbled, "Good. Good to hear. Please tell them I said hi!" I think Isaiah suffered from schizophrenia or some other severe mental illness. I used to see him on the street corner playing the blues on his old, rusted gold saxophone. He stood by his open case with the midnight blue velvet interior and played with all his heart and soul. Periodically, he would stop playing and graciously thank and bless those who tossed a dime or quarter in his torn-up case.

Sometimes he wouldn't show up at the soup kitchen for months. In his absence, I wondered if he was cold or hungry. I wondered if he had a warm place to stay and a pillow to lay his head on. I also thought about who his mother was and how she must have felt when the same baby, whom the nurse placed in her arms at birth, became a grown, unshaven man who spoke nonsense and slept on cardboard boxes on the sidewalks. I wonder if she still looked for him or if she just gave up all hope.

When Isaiah wasn't at the soup kitchen, I found myself driving around the abandoned side streets of the city looking for him. I am not quite sure what I would have done if I found him. I just wanted to know that he was alive.

And then, as if no time would have passed, he walked through the doors of the soup kitchen, with his saxophone case in hand, "Hey, Mary, how have you been? How are your mom and dad? Please tell them I said hi, won't you?"

At this point in my life, I found my faith was becoming my own — not my parent's faith but mine. My experiences with the poor ignited something passionate within me. I was deeply moved by issues of social justice and wanted to meet other people who felt the same. I happened to hear about a Catholic church near where

I was living at the time that had a reputation of serving the poor, and it even had a food pantry.

I went to mass one day. The congregation was vibrant and diverse. There was every race and culture present. And they sang loudly and boldly during the hymns. During the reciting of the Our Father, everyone held hands. Old, young, rich, poor, black, white reached out to hold another's hand and lift them up in heartfelt prayer. It was powerful, and for the first time I felt the electricity of faith run through my body. It was much different than the suburban parish I grew up in. I knew in an instant that I had found my new home.

I am not proud to say this, but it was also the same parish where I gave a nun the finger. Yes, you read that right. A nun. I was in my car on the way to mass, determined to not be late again. The driver ahead of me was puttering along so annoyingly slow, and I was getting more impatient by the minute. So, for the first time in my life, I honked the horn and gave her the finger. It was a confident, poignant nonverbal gesture, a tsunami of repressed emotions. I could see her eyes stare at me in utter disbelief as she peered through the rearview mirror. Then she turned into the same parking lot I was going to, the church parking lot. I followed her in and parked in a space, as far away as I possibly could. Her car door opened oh so slowly as I glanced out my window. A leg with a familiar looking black masculine shoe tied tightly with thin, black laces emerged from the car, then another leg and finally out came a petite woman dressed in a long black habit with a black and white veil on her head. "Oh my God! She was a nun! I just gave the finger to a nun, of all people." Unbelievable. I was doomed to purgatory for sure and that is if I was lucky! I waited until she went into the church then I snuck in the back hoping that she wouldn't recognize me. Yeah, right! Forgive me sister for I have sinned again.

I attended mass there every Sunday and sat in the back pew with all the other people who arrived late. I often found myself staring at the people sitting in the pews in front of me. There were plenty of single people but there were couples, too. With arms embracing one another, they sat. Despite my excitement about my bucket list and trying to feel confident in being single, watching those couples in church made me feel this itty-bitty tiny yearning to be with someone.

So I began to pray. I prayed to St. Anthony, the saint of lost things and missing persons, and then to St. Jude, the saint for the hopeless. I thought that having both saints on my side would not be a bad thing. "Dear Tony. I have lost a man and I don't know where to find him. I need a good Catholic man, one with a sense of humor, deep faith and an intelligent mind. That is all I am asking for. Please hear my prayer." And then, "Dear Judy, Judy, Judy. I hope it is all right that I call you that. I know it sounds like I am referring to you as a woman, but listen, I know you are a man and I know you can help me. I want to find one, a good guy to spend the rest of my life with. I don't want to live life without experiencing this type of love, and I want to have children. Please, St. Jude, consider my cause a worthy one. ... Oh, and if you are offended that I called you Judy, please send me a sign and accept my apologies in advance."

I thought it was worth a shot and, if they didn't come through for me, it is not meant to be, and I was determined to make the best of my life and keep adding to my bucket list.

And then I met him. On a sweltering hot, Sunday morning in August, I walked into mass and happened to notice a handsome man walking behind me. He was clean-cut and nice looking. Dressed in a white buttoned-down shirt and navy casual pants, he appeared confident and very attractive. I had never seen him before because with his looks I would have noticed. I glanced down to his left hand, and I am sure all of the angels and saints above rejoiced with me to the fact that there was no wedding ring. Maybe I needed to revise my bucket list by adding, "Get married."

I lingered in the entryway, pretending to be interested in the fair trade coffee display. With one eye on the coffee and the other eye on him, I saw that he was approaching me. My heart began to race, and I could feel my palms sweating. "Excuse me. Do you know if there is a singles group at this parish?" he asked. Knowing that I was indeed an expert in that area for more years than I cared to mention, I replied, "Why yes. I just happen to be a member. I can introduce you to some people after mass. My name is Mary. What is yours?"

"Nice to meet you," he said. "My name is Michael."

"I can show you where many of the single people sit, and you can join us if you want." As we walked down the side aisle, I glanced up at the murals on the ceiling of all the different saints. I saw the murals of St. Anthony and St. Jude. "Thanks guys," I quietly said to myself.

After mass, Michael asked for my number "just in case he had questions." I dug into my purse to find my business card and when I did, I placed it in his hand. He looked at me with his clear green eyes and asked if I wanted to join him for lunch. A few of my friends were already going out to eat so we decided to meet them at the restaurant. We rode in his little black sports car convertible to the local sandwich place down the street from the church. It was a hot and muggy day. The temperatures rose so fast that the steam was rising from the road like a scene from a scary horror movie. I had worn a cute pair of sandals. They were beige with small blue and purple flowers on them. A silky ribbon tied tightly around my ankle like a delicate ballerina slipper. I felt pretty... until I was getting out of the car. Trying to be lady-like while admiring my beautiful shoes, I gently placed my right foot out of the car and onto the sidewalk. I lifted my shoe up, wanting to take another peek at how cute my shoes were and I felt a slight tug. I tried again to pull my leg up, wondering what could possibly be wrong with my shoe. It was as if I was playing tug of war with a rubber band. Oh my God, I stepped on a piece of sticky pink bubble gum. I tried frantically to break away from the strong pull before Michael noticed but it was too late. He had already come around to my side of the car to see what was taking me so long. Embarrassedly, I looked up at him and shrugged my shoulders in a look of defeat. We both started to laugh. I couldn't hide the family secret. My sister had always told me that the women in our family had a hard time being cool and right she was. I wasn't cool... and that seemed to be okay with Michael. I got out of the car and scraped the bottom of my shoe on the pavement hoping to get the last remaining wad of gum off before I went into the restaurant.

We joined my friends at a long narrow table, and I proudly introduced Michael to them as if I had known him for a very long time. We sat down, ordered our food and as he was talking, I stared at him with utter curiosity. Who was this man? Where did he come from? He spoke about recently moving to Michigan from Rhode Island, finding a new job in the engineering field and an apartment in one of the suburbs of town. As he spoke to my friends, I took in his every word. It looked like he liked my friends and they liked him. Thank you, St. Jude and St. Anthony — another answered prayer. I knew that they would never let me down, no matter how many requests I made or how desperate I was.

After lunch, Michael asked me to show him around the town. We went to a park overlooking the city and stared at the hustle and bustle of the streets below. It was a beautiful sunny day as we walked around the beautifully landscaped grounds.

Later that night, the church softball team that I played on had a game, and I invited Michael to meet me there. Our pastor, Father John was our coach and he insisted that we gather together before the game started to say a prayer. I chuckled under my breath as everyone said "Amen. In the name of the Father, Son and Holy Spirit," because the truth was that we played together as a team for three years and never won a game. In fact, we were so bad that the umpire requested that we contract with a local ambulance service due to the high number of injuries we incurred each week. One practice, as I was standing on the field, I heard my name being called. I glanced over to where the voice was coming from and WHAM — I got hit in the face. My eye bruised immediately. A week later, I was walking into a convenience store, and a woman at the counter asked me what happened. I told her that I got hit with a ball during a baseball game, and she quickly replied, "I've used that excuse before as well."

As usual, our team gathered together that Sunday evening and while holding hands, we prayed. When we said "Amen," I glanced over to the stands and saw Michael. I was so excited to see him but nervous that he would find out that I knew nothing about softball and that actually I was terrified of the ball. The only reason I joined the team was that they were in desperate need for another player — so desperate that they didn't care if I knew how to play or not. But the real reason that I joined the team is that I wanted to go out to eat afterwards to celebrate ... or in our case to mourn.

It was the eighth inning and the score was zero to zero. We were hopeful that we might be able to experience our first win of the season until one of our best players got injured — a hit to the eye. You would have thought that her straw panama hat and her large round black sunglasses would have protected her face but sadly it didn't and she was removed from the game. "Mary. First base," Father John screamed from the sidelines. "Really?" I yelled back. I stood next to the white square pillow on first base and gave an intimidating evil eye to the batter all the while hoping and praying that the ball wouldn't come my way. My brow methodically dribbled sweat down my dirt-covered face as I stood with one hand on my hip and another one in the air, waiting for him to hit the ball. Crack went the bat, and with the speed of lightning, the ball moved through the air in a way that made it look invisible or maybe I needed to clean my sunglasses. I moved to the left and a little to the right, a few steps in front and then a step behind like a dancer in a well-choreographed performance. Squinting through the hot sun's rays trying to detect where the ball actually was headed, I heard a smack and a poof of dirt magically appeared in front of me. When the dust cleared, I saw the white ball roll immediately to the side of me. I could hear the crowds chant my name "Mary! Mary! Mary!" as if we were close to winning the championship game. The pressure was on. I could feel it and as I leant down to pick up the ball; I stepped on my glove and did a somersault in front of everyone. I could hear the crowd inhale a deep breath as I returned to a stand-up position and then as if nothing happened they continued to shout "Mary! Mary! Mary!" By this time I regained my balance, the ball had already went past me and rolled into the outfield. The batter ran to first base, went to second, then third and then to the home plate, scoring the only point of the game. I glanced over at Father John, whose head was bowed down in prayer while doing the sign of the cross.

"You were so close," Michael said as he walked toward me. "Close? Did you see my somersault?" I asked unbelieving that he would think that last move would be considered "close." "Yes, I did. I have never seen anyone do that before." In that very moment, I knew I was in love.

For the first time of my life, I wanted to spend every waking hour with Michael. I thought of him constantly at work, at home and even when I was doing the laundry. And when I was with him, I was giddy like when I was a little girl and had my first crush on Danny O'Leary. One starry night I promised God that I will be good the rest of my life if he let me marry him! Obviously, that didn't happen so I wasn't going to make that mistake twice.

Michael and I talked about everything, our life goals and dreams and everything in between. We attended movies, listened to jazz music in the parks, went to museums and took long walks. He was funny, intelligent and kind, and I loved being with him. As the weeks passed, though, our conversations became more deep and intense. During one phone conversation, he mentioned that he needed to tell me something but he couldn't tell me over the phone. He was adamant that he had to tell me in person. Was he going to break up with me? Was he moving far away? Was he married? Was he gay? Was he a convicted felon or a mass murderer? I read way too many murder mysteries but what could he possibly have to tell me that he could not share on the phone?

He came to my apartment later that night. He knocked on the door and as I opened it, he asked me if I wanted to go for a walk. It was obvious that something was wrong. He seemed different, so serious. As we walked down the steps outside of my 100-year-old apartment building, he said, "There is a fine line between sanity and insanity." I held onto the cold, black iron railing for a moment, reluctant to hear where this story was going. He continued, "I was watching TV last night and one of the main characters was a doctor who suffered with mental illness, bipolar in fact. She couldn't hold it together." We quietly walked down the street to the steps of an old Episcopal church. A large black lantern illuminated the steps as the light from inside the church sprinkled color through the stained-glass windows. Taking my elbow, he guided me to the steps and asked me to sit down with him. I felt nervous not knowing what he was going to tell me. He was acting so odd.

"I need to tell you something so that you can decide whether you want to keep dating me or not. If you don't want to, I totally understand. I just want you to know now so that if you do want to keep dating, I can continue to fall in love with you."

"What is it?"

"About one year ago, I had a nervous breakdown. For months, I couldn't sleep at all. I had too many thoughts racing through my brain every minute of the day and night. When I say 'too many,' it is like 100,000 thoughts competing for my attention, all at the same time. When I focused on one thought, the next one became more powerful that I couldn't remember what the first thought was. It was mind-blowing. And then I heard a deep voice demanding that I get in my car and drive to New Orleans. It was a strong authoritative, almost frightening, voice. So I did, I drove non-stop, from Rhode Island to New Orleans. When I finally made it, I ran out of gas on the side of the highway. A police officer stopped and could tell that something was wrong. I was manic and I was speaking so loud and fast. They call it 'pressured speech.' It was obvious that something was wrong so he took me right away to a psychiatric hospital where I was soon admitted. That is where the psychiatrist diagnosed me with bipolar disorder. I stayed there for about two weeks. He prescribed a few medications and with each day I began feeling a little bit better — my thoughts were clearer and they weren't racing. I didn't hear any voices, only that of my own. The psychiatrist said that he believed that the breakdown was a one-time occurrence because I had been under so much stress at work. He also said that because I recovered so quickly that most likely the diagnosis was mild. I wanted you to know, though."

I was stunned by what he shared and truly at a loss for words. Even though I expected that he would share something about mental illness, I never dreamt that his story would be so scary. I wanted to say the "right" thing, not wanting to offend or hurt him so I quietly muttered, "Is that all?"

"Is that all? Isn't that enough?"

We both busted out laughing. "Yes...that is enough...quite enough. Actually, more than enough," I said.

We walked back to my apartment neither one of us talking. At the steps of my apartment building, he leaned over and kissed me on the lips. I closed my eyes and savored the kiss, not knowing if it would be the last. "Let's take it slow. I need time to process this."

"Sure. Take as much time as you need."

He went home for the evening, and I laid in my bed reflecting on our conversation. I knew a little bit about mental illness from both my undergrad and graduate studies in psychology. During my undergraduate years, I had completed an internship at a local psychiatric hospital. I assisted the social worker in running groups for men who had been diagnosed with bipolar disorder and schizophrenia. It was heartbreaking because I realized that all those men who were on the unit were someone's son, brother, father, uncle. They were someone important to someone. After their life-changing diagnosis, they were treated as if they were inhuman. Teased and taunted, they were called names like "crazy," "insane," "deranged" or words much worse. Families often denied or minimized their illness saying that they just needed to be more responsible and try harder. Some families even disowned them. Instead of calling them by name, the staff at the hospital would speak about them as if their illness was their identity.

"He's *schizophrenic*," a nurse told me about a young man in his 30s who was pacing the floors.

"But what is his name?" I would ask.

This internship frightened me. I heard stories as to how some of the men claimed to see things that no one else saw or believed — that they were God coming back to save the world from evil. Some talked to themselves nonstop, picked fights with others and others rocked back and forth in their chairs as if they were rocking an infant to sleep. We had one man who wore a blue ski cap so that no one could read his thoughts or track his every move. Months later, I saw that man walking the streets of our town. Sometimes he didn't wear the cap, and I knew that he was taking his medications. Other times, he wore his cap and with his shifty eyes, he glanced at other people as if they were out to get him. I knew soon that he would be back on the unit. I used to leave that internship feeling drained, yet thanking God that I didn't know anyone personally who suffered like the men on the unit.

But how could Michael be like those men? He didn't talk to himself; he didn't rock back and forth. He seemed normal to me. After all, the psychiatrist in New Orleans said that it most likely was a one-time occurrence, and it would never happen again. "One more date?" I said to myself. "I think I will go on one more date ... and then break up with him. After all, what would it hurt? He was funny, smart and really nice. Yes, one more date."

And one more date we had ... and another ... and another ... and another.

The whole time we dated I didn't tell many people about our conversation that late night. And when I did, I was very selective as to whom I told and what I shared. I didn't want to hear anyone say, "Are you sure you know what you are doing?" Or "Do you

need to break up with him?" I wasn't ready to break up with him
— not yet.

The first person I told was someone I worked with. She was
a therapist, and we co-facilitated a therapeutic group for parents
who were recently incarcerated. She was compassionate and non-
judgmental. I knew that she struggled with depression and would
most likely understand what he was going through. I purposefully
left out the scary details about his episode and emphasized the
part where the psychiatrist said that he was mild in his diagnosis.
She assured me that many people only experience one episode,
and he sounded like a really wonderful man. She said that she was
so happy for me that I had found someone. I loved her response
but knew that I didn't tell her the whole story.

I then went to the local bookstore and glanced through all
the books on mental illness. The titles were quite daunting but
I continued my search for that one title that would bring me an
ounce of hope for my relationship with Michael. With a cup of
coffee in hand, I sat on the big, old, worn leather couch in the
back of the store and poured through each book. I was on a
mission to find a book that would tell me that everything would
be all right with his illness. I wasn't going to stop until I found it.
So I chose a book with the least frightening title and I read the
first few chapters and then I skipped to the last chapter. It was
so depressing so I put it back on the shelf and tried another one
and then another one. One by one I placed the books back on the
shelf. With a sense of defeat and a tug of depression, I left the
bookstore with my now-cold coffee in hand.

I had to find another source. Those books were mainly written
by individuals who suffered from pretty serious illnesses so the
ones who didn't have a serious diagnosis were out living life and
not writing about the tales of woe. Yeah, that is it. Michael's
illness wasn't as serious as the authors of the books. After all, the
psychiatrist said that his illness was "mild."

At this point, I was ready to test out the news on someone

else. My best friend and I were going out for dinner, and it was the perfect time to tell her about Michael's illness, this time with more detail. She didn't look surprised when I told her about it and all that happened. I left out a few parts like driving manically down south and being hospitalized. Of course, I told her that his psychiatrist thought it was a one-time occurrence and most likely he wouldn't have another episode. I realized as I was saying those words that it was not quite what the doctor said but it sounded good. She listened to me babble on about him. And then she told me about her uncle. She said that he had suffered from bipolar for many years and that throughout all the ups and downs, he and her aunt managed to stay married. She said that it seemed tough at times but they seemed happy together. I left with an ounce of hope.

I then gathered the courage to tell one more friend. We met through work and facilitated a therapeutic group for women who were in domestic violence relationships. She had been through a lot herself and was so grounded in who she was and so compassionate with people who suffered from mental illness. I knew I could trust her so we made a time in which we could meet and talk. I told her what Michael had told me. She listened attentively to my every word. She said that her sister had a friend who was married to someone who was diagnosed with bipolar disorder and she encouraged me to call her.

I waited a few days until I mustered up the nerve to call. My voice was shaking as I told her our story and the details of his illness. She told me how she met her husband and how they finally found out about his diagnosis of bipolar. She said that she and her husband had two young children, and they were afraid that they would inherit the gene. We spoke for hours about her journey and her love for her husband. She said that he chose not to take the prescribed medications because he, too, was diagnosed as mild. Instead, he took different vitamins and fish oil supplements. She said that those natural remedies in addition to exercise helped manage his symptoms. She stated that at times it was difficult but she loved him dearly and that would never have changed her mind about marrying him. Now that was a story I wanted to hear. It was positive and hopeful. I made the decision to continue to date Michael — to be cautious but to allow myself to fall in love, knowing that whatever happened, we could get through anything.

Deep down though, I knew that Michael had a pretty serious diagnosis, but I didn't want to say the words out loud or truly admit it to myself. I quickly learned that if I didn't think about it, I wouldn't have to deal with it. I chose to focus on the positive and not give power to the negative or shed light on the fears that were buried deep within.

One afternoon, Michael called me saying that he left work and that he wasn't feeling well. I asked him what was wrong and all he could say was that he really wanted me to come to his apartment. I said, "Sure, right away," not knowing what was wrong. After 30 minutes of driving and feeling a bit anxious with each minute, I nervously knocked on his apartment door. "Come in," I heard him say. I quietly opened the front door, walked into the narrow dimly lit hallway and into his living room. Michael was sitting on the couch, staring aimlessly into the silence. There was no television on or radio ... just the sound of the clock going tick, tick, tick, tick. I quietly sat down next to him and asked him how he was feeling. He said that he thought that his colleagues at work were reading his mind and laughing at him behind his back. He said that they were watching his every move and reading his emails. He said that they were even monitoring all his doctor's appointments and colluding with the doctors to get information about him. I listened to him talk about how difficult work had been that day, and then he stopped talking. After an hour of silence, I asked him if he minded if I wrote some notes from a therapeutic group I held that afternoon. At first he said sure, but soon after I realized that he was becoming agitated and suspicious. He kept nervously looking at my notes and asking me what I was writing. I told him that I was writing about a client's progress in-group but he insisted that I was writing about him.

"Who are you going to give the notes to? What are you writing in the notes? How do I really know that you are not writing about me and giving those notes to my boss? Are you talking with my co-workers?" he asked hesitantly.

"Michael. I am writing progress notes for the group I ran today. I do it every time I run a group. I promise that I am not writing about you."

"Could you please stop?" he requested.

"Sure," I said. "Of course, I don't have to do this now." I was hurt as to why he was asking me those questions. Doesn't he know me by now? Didn't he trust me?

The clock continued to tick echoing off the white bare walls of his apartment. The stillness was driving me crazy so I suggested that I go out and get dinner. Michael said he was a little bit hungry so I left and drove to a chicken place down the street. I must have been nervous as I ended up buying enough meals to feed the homeless in Detroit. With bags of food in my arms, I returned to the apartment. It was still so quiet you could hear a pin drop. By this time, Michael said that he wasn't hungry, and that he didn't want to eat, so I sat at the dining room table and ate — again in silence while listening to the tick, tick, tick of the clock.

Hours later, Michael said that he was going to call his psychiatrist. He asked me if I would talk with him. Not wanting to make him more agitated, I agreed. He first spoke to the doctor and then handed the phone to me. I had told the doctor that we had only been dating a few months and I didn't know how to help him. The psychiatrist was polite and compassionate and suggested that Michael and I run together. He said that the exercise combined with the increase in medication would help clear his mind and make his paranoid thoughts go away. Running I could do. After all, I had been running for years and I knew that it would be good for both of us.

After hanging up the phone, we laced up our running shoes, left the apartment and started to run. After a few miles, Michael looked at me and said, "I think I feel better." Wow. That was easy, I thought to myself. If this is all his illness is, I can definitely do this. It was that night I realized that I wanted to marry Michael and that together we could make it work — that love was stronger than his illness and if anyone could help him, I would be the one.

Six months from the day we met, Michael asked me out to dinner at a fancy restaurant, where the bathroom was just as beautiful as the dining space. My mom helped me buy a fancy dress for the occasion. It was a black designer dress with a jacket. I had an inkling she was in on the night. Sitting by candlelight, we sipped our wine and talked about our days. After a delicious meal of sirloin steak, baked potato and asparagus, we walked hand in hand down the street toward the center of the town. It was Christmastime and there were a million small white flickering lights hugging the trees on each side of the street. Christmas carols were being pumped over the loudspeaker and horse-drawn carriages carried couples snuggling under the soft, red and black plaid woolen blankets.

As we approached the beautifully decorated gazebo at the center of the town square, Michael knelt down on his right knee, slowly placed his hand in his pants pocket and took out a small black leather box, bound tightly with a silk ribbon. As he opened the box, I saw the most radiant one-carat diamond ring sparkling in the light.

"Mary, will you marry me?"

"Yes. I will marry you. I would love to marry you, Michael."

Much to Michael's chagrin, we decided on a ten-month engagement. Michael wanted to get married right away and questioned why we were waiting so long. I needed time to process all that had happened. In six months, I went from embarking on my bucket list adventures to planning a wedding. It seemed like everything was moving so fast, and he wanted it to go faster. I had so many questions about his illness and wondered how it would affect our lives and wondered if we had children, would they have his illness as well. It became so overwhelming that I stopped thinking and started planning a wedding.

Despite my jitters, we set a date and secured the church and the country club for the reception. We hired a DJ and made a list of our favorite songs. We selected a menu of chicken and roast beef and agreed that any leftovers would be donated to the local homeless shelter. We chose the color scheme of light pink and midnight blue. All the details were coming together. Choosing a dress, asking my bridesmaids, selecting the flowers, designing the centerpieces, attending all of the showers kept us in a swirling whirlwind of activities keeping any probing questions or uneasy feelings at bay.

The day quickly arrived. We shared our vows at the church in which we met. It was a cool, fall September day. The sun was shining bright and the leaves were beginning to change colors from green to red, orange and yellow. The bells in the old stone church tower rang loudly, announcing our nuptials to the world. I made sure I wore something old, something new, something borrowed and something blue. I wanted all of the good luck charms I could get just in case I was getting myself in something that was bigger than I could handle.

My bridesmaids, flower girls and I gathered nervously in the small room below the church. As we waited, we held hands and I prayed. "Dear heavenly Father, I thank you for this beautiful day, for the sacrament of marriage and for the blessing of marrying my best friend. I thank you for my dear friends and family, and I ask you to watch over us as we share our vows and commit to a life and marriage in your name. With this we pray, Amen."

It was time. The pianist began to play and I could hear the angelic sound of our vocalist sing "Ave Maria," each note echoing off the stained-glass windows. We walked upstairs anxiously waiting to walk down the aisle. Michael and his groomsmen, in their black tuxedos entered from the side room, stood in front of the altar and waited for the magnificent oak doors in the back of the church to open. One by one, my bridesmaids walked down the aisle in their long black, strapless gowns and a bouquet of pale pink hydrangeas in their hands. I stood in the back of the church by the Fair Trade Coffee display, the same place I stood when I first met Michael. I held tightly onto my father's arm waiting for the trumpeter to pay the first note of Canon D. As we walked down the aisle, I kept my eyes on Michael.

"I, Mary, take you Michael as my lawful wedded husband, to have and to hold from this day forward. For better or for worse, for richer or poorer, in sickness and in health, to love and to cherish until death do us part."

A FTER A WEEK OF HONEYMOONING in Jamaica, we returned to our lives as a newly married couple. We lived in a two-bedroom apartment on the third floor of a small building. Even though the apartment complex was large, our apartment was like a tree house, privately nestled in the woods.

From our deck, we saw the daily adventures of the chipmunks, squirrels, bunnies and all different types of birds perched on branches. We heard the rain slap the leaves during the storms, the birds chirping to one another throughout the day and, the crickets serenading us all night long. It felt peaceful, cozy and safe inside our humble abode. Yet the apartment complex had quite a disturbing reputation. Soon after we moved in, I began to hear rumors about this "insane" man who murdered his wife in the complex. The mere thought of the rumor sent chills down my spine. I recalled something happening in this suburban town, but it wasn't until I Googled the story, did I find out what really happened. In the early '80s, a young mentally ill man suffered a psychotic breakdown and killed his 20-year-old wife by slashing her throat. That poor woman, I thought to myself. How could she have stayed with him when she knew he was so mentally ill? Why didn't she leave? She must have known he had a severe mental illness. I thought of that story every time I drove into the complex and it left me with trepidation, until I opened the door of our apartment. All seemed safe again!

After we settled back into our jobs and developed a routine, we started to talk about wanting children right away. I was older and had many friends who were infertile so Michael and I agreed to start trying. We took into consideration the genetic component of his illness and researched the statistics. The data indicated that there was a 10 percent chance of our kids having the predisposition for the disorder. Of course, we interpreted the research, as saying there was a 90 percent chance that we would not have a child with a mental illness. So our attempts for conceiving delightfully began.

Within the second month of our marriage, I found out that I was pregnant. I had been feeling extremely fatigued, unmotivated to do anything and the mere smell of anything strong like someone's perfume made me rush into the bathroom. One morning as I was getting ready for work, I decided to take a pregnancy test. Staring shockingly down at the pregnancy test that I held tightly in my hand, I saw the line turn blue. I couldn't believe it so I took another test just in case it was wrong and then another. Stunned with the realization that my life had changed forever and there was no turning back, I slowly walked out of the bathroom like a zombie walking on a deserted street. Michael was in the bedroom getting dressed. I walked up to him and quietly mumbled, "We are pregnant! We are pregnant. We really are pregnant. I'm not kidding. We are pregnant." With each statement, my voice got louder until I was almost screaming. "We are going to have a baby. Oh my God. In nine months, we will have a baby. Oh Lord, what did we do?'" Michael was much more elated with the news — after all he wasn't going to be nauseous, big and fat.

"Oh my God, we are going to have a baby!" He ran over to me, placed his arms around my waist and lifted me up while I whispered in his ear. "I think I am going to get sick."

"We need a house, Mary. Yes. We need to start looking for

a house. This apartment is way too small for the three of us. We won't be able to live here anymore." "Michael, we just moved in here," I pleaded. We had only been in the apartment a few months and the mere thought of packing up again and moving to a new house and a new neighborhood made me mentally collapse with exhaustion. "I feel sick as a dog, Michael. And I don't think we can afford a mortgage right now. I think we need to stay where we are. It is also best financially that we stay here. In time, we will find the right home for our family."

"No, Mary. We need to start looking. I have already called a realtor and we have an appointment to meet with her on Saturday." At this point, I felt that I had no say in the matter. Everything seemed to be moving so fast in my life. It seems like it was yesterday that I was single, and now one and one-half years later I was married, pregnant and looking for a house.

We met with the realtor and told her what we wanted: a small house, four bedrooms preferably, a bathroom on the first floor and a fireplace. Growing up, I had spent many hours in front of our white marble fireplace gazing at the myriad of colors in the fire while writing in my cloth-covered journal. In my mind, a fireplace was non-negotiable.

In addition to going to open houses with our realtor, we spent countless hours driving through different neighborhoods looking at houses. When we weren't doing that or working, we researched property values, school districts and estimated taxes.

House hunting was exhilarating, even though I still didn't think it was the right time to buy. I absolutely loved looking at the different houses, the architecture, inside and out, and the contents. Each house told a story about the neighborhood as well as the people who lived there.

One house, a sprawling red brick ranch, had a huge elk's head mounted on the wall in the entry hall. It scared the living daylights out of me when I walked in and looked into its glassy eyes. Michael looked at me and suggested that we look at another house.

The second house was an adorable pale yellow cottage with a wraparound porch. The outside was pristine but when you walked in, it was a different story. There was so much clutter on the floor we needed a map to walk through. Stacks of newspapers and magazines piled up the walls and the smell was enough to make any person throw up. The dark green laminate counters in the kitchen were layered with grease, and the walls had signs of a mashed potato side dish gone bad. I was good at spotting mashed potatoes on walls because the first time I cooked them in graduate school, I didn't cook them all the way. So when I used the mixer, potatoes went flying everywhere: the cabinets, the walls and even the 10-foot-tall ceilings. I felt a little guilty when I moved out of the apartment because the potatoes remained.

The one thing that was consistent with our search was each time we entered a house, Michael warned me not to act too excited as he felt that it would influence the realtor and the selling price. With an unenthused affect, I looked at each room, verbally reciting the pros and cons as if I were a real estate agent myself. And then I walked into what was the baby's room. It made my heart ignite with joy realizing that we were going to have a baby. Michael would quietly walk up behind me, place his hands on my shoulders and whisper in my ear, "Dear Lord, please bless our family as we await the arrival of our baby. Keep us safe on this journey. Amen." I collected myself by breathing deeply and brushing away the tears just before the realtors came in the room. "I'm not sure if this room is big enough," as I winked at Michael. We then continued the tour.

This pastime of looking at houses continued for a few months and then we decided to put the search on hold to celebrate our first Christmas together, Michael, myself and our baby-to-be.

One night, Michael came home from work and surprised me with a live Christmas tree, one that he bought at the local nursery. It was tall and thin, and much different than the trees I grew up with.

In my family, we drove to a tree farm out in the country, cut down the biggest and fattest tree that we could find and lugged it home. My dad would place the "damn tree," as he fondly referred to it, in the tree stand that was attached to a large piece of wood. Dad made the stand specifically so that our trees would not tumble over once we got it in the stand. It was a tradition that Dad put the lights on the tree while we sat on the couch listening to Christmas carols on the stereo. Each year, Dad would approach his responsibility with utter seriousness. He carried the tall wooden ladder into the living room, and carefully positioned it by the tree. With one hand on the already lit strands of lights and another on the ladder, he made his ascent. With a look of fierce determination, he carefully climbed each step until he slammed his head on the ceiling. We knew it was going to happen because he did it every year. "DAMN. Who picked out this damn tree?" We knew not to say a word so we sat side by side listening to Christmas carols and waiting for his descent from the ladder and into the family room. My siblings and I didn't let it damper our festivities for the evening, it was just part of the annual tradition.

Even though the tree Michael brought home was much smaller than the ones I was used to, it was pretty and he didn't even cuss when he put on the lights. We took out our individual boxes of ornaments and with each one, we told the story of who gave it to us and what it meant to us. I told most of the stories. "I made this one when I was five years old. We used a paintbrush to put glue on it and then we dipped it in glitter."

When all the ornaments were hung, we sat side by side on the couch listening to soft Christmas music. With his arm over my shoulder and my hand on my tummy we stared with utter amazement at all the blessings in our lives.

Christmas came and went, and I was really beginning to show. By February, Michael insisted on resuming house hunting.

He was more persistent than ever in buying a house before the baby arrived. It wasn't as fun as it was in the beginning because I was getting bigger, and it was difficult for me to get in and out of the car. I kept trying to postpone the search but his mind was made up and nothing I said would change that. One sunny yet cold day, we rode with our realtor to different neighborhoods. As we were driving down an old street, I saw my house. It was a small barn-red Cape Cod with black shutters and a long driveway that led to a picket-fenced backyard. It was quaint and adorable and I knew it was mine. We parked on the side of the road while I stared and said, "This is it!" Michael once again lectured me as to not showing my excitement, so with a stiff upper lip and a blank stare, I got out of the car and walked up to the house. The owners were in the driveway as we walked up to them and asked if we could see the house. They were eager to sell it so they invited us in. We walked into an eat-in kitchen with a small family room to its side. The kitchen was perfect with cherry wood cabinets and black and white granite counter tops. I knew immediately that this home was a good home — I just had that feeling. The house was just what we wanted: four bedrooms, a full-size bathroom on the first floor and another one on the second floor and a beautiful tan tile wood-burning fireplace. By this time, I was ecstatic about this house but I tempered my enthusiasm as we walked through each room. As we finished the tour, we looked into each other's eyes, smiled and then returned to the stiff upper lip. Within 24 hours we became homeowners. Although it still seemed fast. I loved our new home and I was so excited to make it our own.

The closing date was a few months away so we had ample time to pack up our belongings. In the evenings and on weekends, we went room-to-room carefully wrapping each item and placing it in a box. Michael began to take a lot of time off. I was nervous as to how much time he was taking off work but I convinced myself that it was because it was our first house and he wanted everything to be perfect. He became obsessed with packing the apartment during the day and he went nightly to the new house, shampooing the carpet, painting some walls and scrubbing the kitchen floors. He spent many nights there cleaning into the wee hours while I stayed at the apartment. Our money dwindled away as he purchased cleaning supplies and other new items for our house. I was already cautious about the money, so this heightened my anxiety to an almost boiling point.

One night after I glanced at all the mounting receipts and the stack of bills, I could feel that I was going to explode. I didn't want to cause him any undue stress as I already suspected that his illness was peeking its ugly head into our lives. I left the house, got into the car and just started driving. I drove into the country on the dark winding roads. With the windows down and the music blaring, I was finally able to breathe and think. It was the first time I questioned whether I made the right choice in marrying Michael. Lately he seemed so distant from me and not interested in our pregnancy. He was consumed and trapped in his own spiraling thoughts. And then THUD. I ran over something. At first, I didn't know what it was but then I looked in my rearview mirror and saw the dead body of a black cat. I immediately pulled to the side of the road and with my hands cupping my head, I sobbed. I sobbed for the cat, I sobbed for Michael, I sobbed for me, and I sobbed for our baby. I sobbed for the life that I wanted and the life that I had. With my eyes swollen, I drove back to our apartment and fell asleep on the couch while Michael stayed at the empty house, cleaning.

A week later we moved into our little red house. Many of our friends came over to help us unpack the boxes and transform our house into our home but one person was missing, and that was Michael. He was there in body but he was absent in his presence. He mechanically brought the boxes in and placed them in the rooms but he didn't talk to anyone, including me. I tried to compensate for his lack of conversation by talking non-stop but our friends still noticed that something was different with

Michael. In the days to come, he became more withdrawn, spending time putting things together, and later reading religious books or playing on the computer. As weeks turned into months, he began walking around the house agitated and talking about never having any thoughts to himself. He said that while he was at the hospital when he was first diagnosed, they planted a chip in his brain so that all his thoughts could be broadcast for others to hear.

As I was planning the arrival of our firstborn, he was mumbling about the FBI watching him. While I was decorating the baby's room, he was walking around making sure no planes where flying over our house tracking his every move and reading his thoughts. As he withdrew into his world, I withdrew into mine making myself believe that everything would be alright. But I knew, deep down, that it wasn't.

Weeks before the baby's arrival, Michael started coming home from work earlier each day telling his boss that he had to do errands or pick up things for the house. My heart stopped every afternoon when I pulled into the driveway and saw his car parked there. I was so afraid that he lost his job or was on the way to losing his job. I ranted and raved about being responsible at work and making good choices. I even threw the guilt card in by saying that "my dad would never have done anything like that." My words had no effect whatsoever. He became more convinced in his own convictions, and the more I begged, the more he became quiet and withdrawn into himself.

With clearer eyes, I began to do more research on mental illness. I noticed that there was a link to a website for families who love someone who suffers with mental illness. The agency had support groups in my town. The website said that it was a nonprofit, grassroots, self-help, support and advocacy group. That sounded like it was something for me.

After Michael left for work, I dialed the number for the local chapter. I spoke with a man who ran the monthly group. I told him that I was recently married and that my husband had been diagnosed with bipolar a few years earlier. I told him that I was fine but I was just interested in learning more. He shared his story with me about his son who was diagnosed with severe schizoaffective disorder. He spoke about the fear of sharing what was happening with others at that time, and the isolation he and his wife felt as a couple. He said that they yearned to find others who were in similar situations so that they would not feel so alone in this heart-breaking journey. I was touched by his honesty and saddened by his story. At the end of the conversation, he invited me to attend the monthly gathering. And I agreed.

The meeting was on a Wednesday night and the group met in a large conference room in a local hotel. I was anxious as I drove there trying to convince myself that Michael wasn't that sick and most likely I would get nothing out of the meeting but there was something inside of me that knew I needed help and support.

The automatic doors abruptly opened to the lobby. There was a sign with the words "Support group" and an arrow pointing to the beige narrow hallway to the left. I hesitated, thinking that I might not be ready for such a meeting but I continued to walk down the hall. I entered the small meeting room. There were gray metal folding chairs arranged in a circle. Coffee was percolating in the back of the room and a cluster of men and women gathered around in tight circles, talking to one another while clutching on to the white Styrofoam coffee cups. A gentleman, standing in the front of the room, noticed my awkwardness and walked toward me. With his hand reaching out to mine, he said "Hi. My name is Bill. Is this your first time here?"

"Yes. Can you tell? My name is Mary. I am a bit nervous, and I am not sure why I am really here. My husband has bipolar but he is doing well." Bill stared at my teary eyes, and I knew that he knew that I was not fine.

"I felt the same way when I came to this room about ten years ago," he said. "I was nervous, really nervous, and I questioned why

I was here. I thought that my wife and I could do it on our own and that love would make everything better but it didn't. The one thing I ignored was her illness and the severity of it. The more I denied it, the more I allowed it to steal from me, my happiness, my hopes, my dreams and all that I wanted for us as a couple and as a family. I knew that I had to be honest with what was going on, no matter how difficult and painful it would be. So I attended one meeting and then eventually another and then another."

As he finished talking, I had the urge to run out of the meeting room, down the hall and into the safety of my car. But the room filled up quickly blocking my exit. Bill extended his hand and said, "I am so glad that you came Mary. If you need anything else, please call me or stay after group and we can talk."

"Thanks, Bill, so much!"

The meeting began and stories were shared, stories of wild manic episodes, extravagant spending sprees, dangerous drug use and doing time in the "pen." It was all too scary for me because Michael wasn't like that. He was different, and I knew that together we could combat this illness and keep it under control. He just needed rest, and everything would go back to normal, at least I thought. I left the meeting feeling so sad for the other families who had to go through so much but I convinced myself that their world was so different than ours.

As the baby's due date quickly approached, Michael seemed to get better. He had gone to the psychiatrist and they increased his medication. When he wasn't there, he was at the therapist's office. All in all, Michael was excited about having a baby, and he kept asking me how I was feeling. I kept reassuring him that everything was fine and I was just having a few uncomfortable contractions. Finally in the middle of a hot summer night, the contractions took my breath away, and I knew I was in labor. Michael was fast asleep so I nudged him and whispered, "I think it is time, honey. I think the baby is coming." He jumped out of bed and threw on some clothes as I waddled behind, cramped over and engulfed in excruciating pain. The contractions were coming fast and hard as we drove above the speed limit to the hospital. It was dark outside and no one was around as we entered the front doors. We were so cocky during our Lamaze class thinking that we would be naturals at this whole delivery thing but at that moment, we couldn't even remember where the labor and delivery unit was, not a good sign. Wandering around the hospital, screaming and stopping dead in my tracks as the contractions became stronger, we finally stumbled upon a nurse who was able to direct us to the right floor. Once we arrived on the floor, the nurse reviewed our birth plan.

"So your birth plan says that you want to go natural."

"*HELL NO!*" I screamed. "*I need drugs and I need them now! Michael, tell them I need drugs NOW!*"

He looked at the nurse and with fierce determination he said, "She definitely needs drugs, *now*. Please give her drugs."

One nurse frantically wheeled me down the hall in the wheelchair, around the corner, through the double doors into the labor and delivery room. Another nurse was waiting there to help me out of the wheelchair into the bed. She glanced at her clipboard and says, "So you want to go natural, right?" Michael and the other nurse looked at her in outrage and at the same time they yelled, "*No! She wants drugs.*" I never wanted an IV more than I wanted this one. Shortly after the epidural, I returned to myself. It was as if instantly I transformed from a raging werewolf into an excited mother waiting the birth of her child. And of course everyone in the room was ecstatic and grateful that I had calmed down.

Within a few hours of drug-induced euphoria, Leo was born. Seven pounds eight ounces with thick black hair that probably could have been cut months ago. It was love at first site, and as I saw Michael look into Leo's eyes, I knew everything would be okay, or at least it had to be okay. We had a child now who needed us and depended on us, who gave us purpose.

Michael stayed at the hospital with Leo and I. He was so attentive all night. As soon as Leo cried, he picked him up and brought him over to me. One of the night nurses came up to me and said, "You are so lucky to have such a nice husband." I nodded in agreement. I was thankful for his help and his love but I was worried that he wasn't getting any sleep. I knew with his illness, he definitely needed sleep. I kept urging him to go home and get some rest, but he refused saying that he wanted to be with Leo and me. The next day we drove home, one happy but tired family.

"There is a fine line between sanity and insanity." Michael always said that, and I knew that he was quickly approaching that line. Both of us were not sleeping, and we were cranky. I tried to talk about Leo but the conversations ended up being about his work. He was convinced that his colleagues had access to his medical records and called him "crazy" behind his back. He said that they were watching him and listening to his conversations, making it hard for him to concentrate and do his work. He was convinced that his manager was plotting against him, trying to get him fired. Each morning it became more difficult for him to get up, and it seemed anguishing for him to stay at the office for a full eight hours. He always had a reason to come home early despite my pleas for him to stay. But when he did stay, he came home looking utterly exhausted.

I tried to be supportive while juggling the insatiable needs of a newborn. The books always recommended napping while the baby was sleeping but I used the time to catch up with the chores and laundry so Michael didn't feel overwhelmed when he came home. When I wasn't doing chores, I was breastfeeding. And when I wasn't breastfeeding, I was doing chores. Having an infant was so much more time-consuming than I had ever dreamed, and what used to be my normal was no longer important. Instead of dressing nicely and dabbing perfume on my wrist, I walked around smelling like puke and dirty diapers. Whereas before, I put on makeup and got dressed up to go out and do errands. After Leo arrived, I would drive to the local pharmacy in my pink robe and bunny slippers to pick up diapers.

I even think Leo soaked up my stress like an over-saturated sponge because he would scream for hours upon end. I did everything to try to calm him down like taking long walks, carrying him around in a baby backpack and even singing to him. Reluctantly he would fall asleep just to awake with the slightest of sound. It seems like I was always walking on eggshells afraid to wake either Michael or Leo. I was exhausted and irritable all the time. Even the all-nighters in grad school didn't compare to this.

As the weeks went on, I could tell that Michael was getting sick again. He insisted that he was fine but I knew deep down that he wasn't. It didn't seem like anything I was doing was really helping him.

After the one-month visit to the pediatrician, we were driving back home. "Do you see that license plate?" he asked.

"Which one?"

"That one," he said pointing to the car in front of us. "I think it is trying to tell me something. It's a code."

"That license plate?" I questioned.

"Yes. They all have hidden meaning and they are telling me to do things."

"Like what?"

"Never mind" he said. At that point, I just wanted to cry. I knew that his paranoia was coming back and there would be no rest in sight.

As the days passed, Michael became more introverted and spent a great deal of time reading religious books. His eyes were distant and cold as he withdrew from our family. He also stopped eating and was losing weight fast. He said he was "fasting for religious reasons." Leo and I had a routine by this point, but I could tell that there was a storm brewing ahead. Michael would continue to leave work early for different reasons. He told his boss that he needed to help with the baby, or pick up things for me yet in fact, he came home and retreated into the office. I tried to do everything that would make this stage of our lives less stressful for him, hoping that his symptoms would in time be reduced. Yet in the deepest moments of stillness, I knew that Michael was crossing the line between sanity and insanity and there was nothing I could do about it. Again, I asked him if he was taking his medications and he, in an aggravated tone of voice, insisted that he was. I found myself counting his medications and walking in the kitchen as he was taking his medications to see if he was really swallowing them. I didn't want to be a medication Nazi but I was becoming one for fear of what could happen next.

After spending an afternoon shopping with Leo, I drove

home and saw Michael's car parked in the driveway. I immediately thought that he had been fired. I took Leo's car seat out and walked in the back door. Michael was sitting in the living room. With his head down, he looked as if he was deep in thought. He didn't even notice that I had walked in the door. And then I heard his quiet voice, "I need to go to the hospital, Mary." Relieved in a way that he was asking for professional help, I instinctually went into action. I mentally created a list of what we needed to do to go down to the hospital. Leo was sleeping in the car seat so I gently put him down near Michael. I walked into our bedroom and pulled out the luggage we bought for our honeymoon. I then opened his dresser drawer and pulled out some underwear, undershirts, a few pair of jeans and a few clean shirts and threw them in the suitcase. I tossed in his toothbrush, toothpaste and his shaving kit. And before closing it, I placed in a picture of Leo after he was born. I wanted to remind Michael of why he needed to get well, for Leo, for me, for our lives together.

It was dark by the time we drove to the hospital. Leo slept soundly in his car seat. Within a few minutes of being in the emergency room, Michael was admitted to the psychiatric unit. A nurse in her blue scrubs met us at a door on the eighth floor. At first, she said that we couldn't bring Leo in the unit but I begged telling her that I was breastfeeding, and we weren't prepared to leave him with anyone else. Reluctantly, she agreed. We followed her in, and I heard the door lock behind us. It was a hollow locking sound. She ushered us into a small room with white walls, a white table and three muddy colored metal chairs. She said that the staff was getting his room ready, and they would need me to complete the paperwork. She handed me some forms, and with a pen in my shaking hand, I responded to the questions the best I could while she took Michael back to his room.

While we were waiting, I watched patients pace down the narrow halls, muttering nonsensical words under their breath. One woman with dirty long brown hair framing her pale complexion sat in a fetal position in the corner of the "activity" room, rocking back and forth in a catatonic state. Another man shuffled on the floor in his navy-blue corduroy slippers and spoke about aliens from outer space that abducted him in the middle of the night. Joseph, an older man in his 70s was different though. Holding a CD in his hand, he walked gingerly around the halls singing. I could hear a faint voice in the back room saying "Shut up! Can't anyone make him shut up?" It didn't bother him, and it didn't interrupt his performance either. He sang his songs until he saw Leo and I. "Do you want my CD? I sang all of the songs on it myself." I inquisitively looked at him wanting to say, "Can't you see I am struggling here? My husband was just admitted and you are asking me if I want a CD?" Immediately, I felt guilty for merely thinking those thoughts — after all he was a patient, too, and God only knows how long he has been on the unit. "Sure. I would love one. Thank you." Pleased, he handed it to me, and walked away singing.

Janet, our nurse, came out of Michael's room and walked toward me. She asked if I wanted to go back to where he was. I did. Michael was sitting on the bed, staring at the white linoleum floors. "Michael has something he wants to tell you," Janet said. Taking in a deep breath, I said, "Okay."

In a colorless tone of voice, he began, "I was driving around today looking for a gun. I drove all over and I went into different stores."

"Why were you looking for a gun?" I asked, scared to hear the answer.

"I wanted to shoot myself, Mary. I can't live like this anymore. The thoughts won't go away. I have tried but I can't stop listening to them."

My eyes grew bigger and filled with tears of sadness and then tears of anger. "You were going to kill yourself? You have a wife who loves you dearly and a two-month-old son. He needs his dad. He needs you, Michael. *I NEED YOU!*"

The nurse interrupted my emotional wrath by suggesting that we talk further tomorrow. I breathed deep again, pushing a pause button on my pain. I couldn't believe what I had just heard. This wasn't supposed to be like this. We just got married a year ago, and we just had a healthy baby boy. How could Michael think about doing this to Leo, to me? Was he going to kill himself at home? Was I supposed to find him? Would Leo see his body? What did he expect me to say to our son about why he does not have a father? How would that affect Leo?

It was about midnight and the nurse came up to me and gently placed her arms around my shaking, defeated shoulders. In a soft voice, she recommended that Leo and I go home and get some sleep. She said that Michael would do the same and that we could see him the next morning. I reluctantly agreed. I didn't want to leave Michael but I was exhausted by this point and just wanted to go home. I wanted to close my eyes and pretend that this never happened.

As I picked up Leo's car seat and exited the door, I heard a clicking of the door locking behind me. I immediately had a flashback of when I was an intern in the psychiatric hospital. I was sitting in the sterile waiting room as I watched an older gray-haired man leave the unit. The door locked behind him. He lifelessly turned around facing the door and looked through the rectangular wire-meshed glass window. Slowly he placed his wrinkly right hand on the window as his wife who was behind the lock door did the same. Their grief screamed loud by their mere touch of their hands. Not only were they separated by a glass window, separated by a locked door but separated by mental illness. And now, a locked door separated my husband and me.

Dazed, I drove home and crawled into our queen-sized bed with Leo sleeping soundly in my arms. Watching him sleep, I began to breathe in sync with his baby breath. I dozed off to sleep until the loud ringing of the phone next to my bed pierced the silence. I quickly picked it up in hopes to not wake up Leo. It was six o'clock in the morning and it was the first time he slept through the night. I wanted him to sleep as long as he could.

"Mary?" I heard Michael's voice, "I love you!"

"I love you too, Michael. I am so sorry that you are sick. We will get through this, I promise you. I don't know how but I know that we will get through it."

"I know we will, Mary," and he hung up. I placed the phone back on the dresser, looked at Leo and fell back to sleep.

A few hours later, I received a call from the nurse stating that Michael was checking himself out of the hospital, against medical advice. Michael's reasoning was that he "didn't belong on the unit with all of those crazy people." I completely understood what he was saying but at the same time, I had felt some sense of relief knowing that trained physicians and nurses were observing him. In some ways, his hospitalization gave me a needed break. I was exhausted beyond words and just wanted to sleep. He hadn't even been evaluated for new medications. Why couldn't they make him stay although I know that when Michael has something in his mind, there was no stopping him.

I got Leo and I dressed, and we headed down to pick up Michael. We took the elevator to the eighth floor and waited for the door to be unlocked so that we could go in. The nurse handed me some paperwork and said that she didn't recommend this. I nodded in agreement but knew that there was no convincing Michael otherwise. I signed him out, and we walked back to the car. We didn't say much on the way home. There wasn't much to say. I was still exhausted from the night before but I knew that I had to be vigilant and keep my eye on him at all times. Even though he said that he was not suicidal, I was terrified that he had a plan and that this time he would follow through with it. I checked the closets and in the basement for any guns or knives that he could have hidden. I didn't find anything, except the BB gun he used when he was a young boy. I took it out of the box in the basement and hid it in another one so that he couldn't find it. The mere sight of the gun made me nauseous.

While Michael called his work to discuss taking six weeks of short-term disability, I stayed busy picking up his new prescriptions, taking care of Leo, cleaning the house, making meals and, out of the corner of my eye, watching Michael's every move. The busier I kept myself, the less I felt the horrifying feelings of what just happened. He was granted the time off, and I was so relieved. I had high hopes that with each week, he would begin to feel better and return to the man I married. But in fact, his paranoia was still winning the battle of his mind. He hated being near the phone because he thought people could hear our conversations, even if we were not even on the phone. He even called our friend, John, who worked for the phone company, and asked him if it was possible for someone to have their phone lines tapped. Without knowing that Michael was sick, John said yes. With that comment, Michael was convinced that his work had tapped our lines, were listening to our every word and plotting to "get rid of him at work." Nothing I said would persuade him otherwise. He remained pensive and always suspicious. He even refused to sit outside for fear that the planes that were flying over our house were tracking his every move and his every thought. It was like something out of a movie, so surreal and yet it was my reality, my life. Even though I was getting used to his symptoms and I knew that I couldn't talk rationally to someone who was not rational, I was saddened by watching him fade away into his illness. He was much thinner but he still looked the same, yet the man I married and who was my friend was gone. I felt sick inside knowing that there was nothing I could do to help him feel better or take his illness away. I was in a constant state of sorrow, pulled by the never-ending tug of depression. I wanted desperately for our lives to be different but I was coming to grips that his illness was a huge part of our marriage. I could either learn to accept it or

I could leave. I loved Michael though, and I knew that I couldn't leave him when he needed me the most.

The psychiatrist had told Michael, that it would take about four to six weeks for a new medication to take effect. I crossed off each day on the calendar hoping and praying that with each day, our lives would become easier. They didn't.

"People are watching me, Mary," he said, as he peered through the small window in our front door. "I know they are spying on us."

"No one is spying on us, Michael," I tried to reassure him. "We are not that interesting of a couple for someone to take time out of their day to watch our comings and goings and listen to our conversations. I just can't see that happening. Let's go to bed, Michael, please."

He turned away from the front door, and I saw tears streaming down his face. No matter how hard I tried to rationalize it, he truly believed that people were watching us. It was heartbreaking to see his deep despair. The thoughts in his mind were real to him no matter how ridiculous they sounded to me. I motioned him to sit on the couch with me. He did, we held hands and we both just cried. He was crying because he was afraid someone was going to hurt us, and I was crying because I knew he was crossing that fine line again. With a little bit of nudging, I encouraged him to call the psychiatrist. He did and he was told to take another pill and go to bed. The psychiatrist reassured us that things would be better in the morning. I just wanted the night to end so I checked on Leo who was still asleep and then I crawled into bed.

Within hours I woke up and Michael wasn't in bed. I went into the living room to check him, and there he was asleep on the couch. I gently placed a quilt over his body, kissed him on the forehead and sat in the rocking chair watching him sleep. How could something so horrifying happen to such a great man? Why was it happening to us? It was as if the person I married only stopped by for short visits while the man who was sick stayed around for longer periods of time.

Michael took some more time off work and slept a lot. Slowly, so very slowly, he began to return to a normal routine and went back to work. I worked hard to keep life at home peaceful which was hard with an infant. I maintained the house, did the laundry, baked cookies from scratch and had dinner on the table at five. I still worked and ran therapeutic groups but I tried to get friends to help take care of Leo during those times so Michael didn't have to stress out and struggle.

Life had been unexpectedly stable for nine months when I found out that I was pregnant again. It was Easter day and we had Michael's and my family over for brunch. Leo was excited that the Easter bunny came to our house. Sporting his pink Easter bunny sunglasses and his pale blue shorts, white cotton shirt and a blue bow tie with a blue bunny on it, he was carried like a king to his table. Everyone brought something to share so all I had to do was bake the ham. Compulsively piercing holes in the ham, I stuffed it with the strongly aromatic cloves. It was a new recipe, and I wanted to dazzle his family with my culinary abilities. Instead I dazzled myself. The smell steaming from the oven made me sick to my stomach.

"You are glowing," my mom said. "You must be pregnant."

I gasped. "Oh God no. I am not pregnant. " Michael and I looked at one another with big eyes wondering what she knew that we didn't. We finished with dessert while everyone dawdled around outside on the deck talking about the weather, upcoming vacations and work. When the sun began to set and when everyone left, I immediately went into the linen closet and pulled out a pregnancy test. I waited anxiously for the results. She was right. I was pregnant.

I WAS EXCITED TO BRING ANOTHER child into our world but I was worried as to how another child would affect Michael's illness. He always wanted a large family but I knew how much we struggled with his illness with one child. I had no clue what it would be like with two, only sixteen months apart. We had such a rocky start and I had the funny feeling that the landscape would end up being more treacherous.

As each month passed, I grew bigger and bigger and fell more in love with this precious baby growing inside of me. I soaked in the moments that I was able to stop and place my hand on my belly just in time to feel her kick. I called her "thumper" because she would have fistfights with my stomach and I witnessed each fight. Even though she felt like an alien in my tummy as she moved around, she was truly a blessing, and I was excited to meet her.

During this time, Michael changed jobs. He said that everyone in the engineering field changed jobs frequently, and he wanted to be closer to home to help with the kids. I supported him but was wondering deep down if he was leaving his job because he was getting paranoid again. As soon as that thought appeared, I shoved it away. He mentioned a few times how he felt that no one liked him at work and that he thought that they were talking about him behind his back but he still managed to go to work every morning and work a full day. He came home chipper and ready to get on the ground and play with Leo. I felt a little bit hopeful or maybe I just escaped into the bubble of denial, at least for the day.

Lucy arrived weighing 6 pounds and 5 ounces, beautiful, healthy and totally bald. This time my birth plan clearly stated that I wanted and needed an epidural. There was no confusion because I think the nurses remembered me. Michael and I called our family and friends to tell them that I was in labor and eight hours later, Lucy was born. She had deep blue eyes, revealing the depth of her soul as if she had been around longer than any one of us.

Her entrance in our lives turned out to be more than an extra car seat. It was the juggling of the needs of a rambunctious toddler, a crying newborn and a mentally fragile husband. As soon as I got Lucy to sleep, Leo was up pulling all the plastic bowls out of the kitchen cabinets, flushing toy cars down the toilet and dumping all of the Cheerios on the living room floor. If I wasn't changing a diaper, feeding a hungry child, calling the plumber, I was chasing Leo all the while trying to keep our home stress free. Taking a nap was a luxury, one that I never experienced. I would look in the bathroom mirror and not even recognize myself. With bags under my eyes, and hair not combed for days, I ran around like a chicken without its head and that was not an attractive sight.

Michael's symptoms began to show up again. He was coming home early from another new job. He stopped eating and was losing a lot of weight. No matter how hard I tried to shield him from the stress, nothing seemed to work. I dreaded with all my soul what was ahead of us.

One morning, he got up and got ready for work. His face was unshaven and his hair was dirty and uncombed. He wore an old undershirt — the same one he wore for painting projects around the house. There were different paint splotches all over and there were holes under his arm. He had on his tattered work jeans with holes in the knees.

"You can't go to work like that!" I said.

He was short with me and in an angry tone of voice, he said "Mary, let go of it. Everyone wears this and it is dress-down day. I can wear what I want and you can't tell me otherwise."

"But Michael," I pleaded. "You have holes in your T-shirt, they can't possibly condone that."

He left and slammed the door making the old windows shudder. I could hear him get in the car and speed out of our long driveway. He was gone.

I continued with our routine not knowing what would happen next but sensing that something terrible was right around the corner. I was anxious as I fed the kids, and played with them on the floor, waiting for a call from his employer saying that something happened.

And then Michael called. His voice was hushed, guarded and suspicious sounding. "Mary, is that you?"

"Yes. It's me. What's wrong?"

"Everyone is whispering about me. They are trying to get me fired," he said.

"Michael, I think you are getting sick again. I think you need help."

"Mary. I can't do this anymore. I yelled at my boss and demanded that he stop reading my thoughts. And I can hear voices in my head, Mary. It is like 50 people are surrounding me talking at the same time, although I can't see them. They are screaming at me, Mary! There are so many, I can't understand what they are saying?" And then, I could hear him crying. "Mary, you have to help me."

I breathed in deep, "Okay. We will get through this. Listen to me. Where are you now?"

"I am in the hallway. I know they are watching me now, and I know they can hear me, but it is the only place I could call you."

"Walk down to the front lobby and wait there for me. I am leaving the house now and will call you as soon as I get there. I will be there as soon as I can. Don't worry — we can get through this. You will be okay. I promise. Do you understand what I am saying?"

"Yes," he said. "I will go downstairs, and wait for you."

"Good. Don't leave. If you need to walk, just walk back and forth in the lobby but don't leave the office. I will be there as soon as I can."

I immediately hung up the phone and dialed my friend Amy. She could hear the fear in the sound of my voice and said that she would come over right away to watch the kids. I changed their diapers, got them snacks and waited for Amy to come to the house. As soon as she knocked on the door, I ran out and got in the car. I prayed for his safety, my sanity and that we would get through the next hurdle. As I pulled into the parking lot, he came out of the building. I opened the door for him and helped him in. At this point, I felt disconnected from all emotion. I was in crisis mode and began making a list in my mind as to what I needed to do next.

"Where did you park the car?" I asked him gently.

"Over there," pointing to the lot on the left.

"Okay. Wonderful. After I drop you off at the house, Amy, the kids and I will go down and pick up the car and bring it home. I need you to call your boss and tell him that you are ill and that you had to go home. And then call the psychiatrist. He will tell us what to do next."

When we got home, Michael went directly into the bedroom. I could hear him pacing back and forth. I begged him to call the psychiatrist but he refused, saying that he just needed to calm down. "Don't leave the house please. We will be back as soon as we can. Stay here though, Michael, please."

Amy and I packed the kids in the van and headed to his office building. I felt guilty leaving him at the house, and I was worried that he wouldn't stay there but I knew that he wasn't fit to drive and there were only enough seats for the kids, Amy and I.

I felt good checking this off my list, but I knew that when I returned home, I had to deal with the reality of his illness. It was so much easier to make a list of all the things I needed to do rather than sit and wait for his symptoms to go back in hiding again, at least for a while. Michael took more time off work. I was relieved to have him home where I knew he was safe, and I could monitor his symptoms. I tried to stay busy with taking care of the kids so I wouldn't question every word he said wondering if it was paranoia. Friends came over and picked up the kids to go on play dates so that I could take a break as well. I was exhausted emotionally and physically from everything we had gone through. My chest tightened with anxiety and I had to push the pause button again ... pushing my emotions down deeper and deeper beyond reach.

Life got a little better with time, but not much better. There was a period of a few months, where Michael seemed normal; going to work and coming home playing with the kids. I was vigilant looking for any signs of his illness. He changed jobs again, and he seemed to be happy ... for a while. We became pregnant with our third baby, another girl. Nine months flew by and Michael seemed to be doing well.

Elisabeth was born in May weighing 8 pounds 7 ounces. She had long black hair and chubby cheeks. When Leo and Lucy came to the hospital to see her, they were elated with joy. Their laughter and enthusiastic questions filled the halls and also my heart. "Is she coming home with us?" "Can I hold her, please mommy?"

I couldn't believe that we had three beautiful children who would grow up together and hopefully be close friends. We were finally a family, one that I dreamt of since childhood.

Adjusting to three young children was a little bit more challenging than I had thought. Not only were the diapers expensive but I also seemed to be always wiping someone's bottom, cleaning up milk off the floor or acting as a referee. Elisabeth had colic and for a few hours every night, she screamed her head off. The witching hour was 5 p.m. and I was the one who tried to calm her down. I rocked her, massaged her body and put her car seat on the dryer but nothing worked. She still screamed until her face was red and she was barely able to catch her breath. The more she wailed, the more stressed I became. I knew that Michael was lacking on sleep, and I knew how essential sleep was to keep his illness at bay. I tried so desperately to keep everyone quiet while he was at home but that was nearly impossible. Her cries would become more inconsolable. I walked with her in a baby pack; I even drove in the country hoping that the sound of the humming engine would calm her down. It did but as soon as we got back to the house and got out of the car, she started to wail again. When I accepted another contract job, I knew I had to get someone to watch Elisabeth, especially since she was colicky in the evenings. I couldn't depend on Michael to do it.

I had a good friend who was a nun that lived in a local convent. She, and the other nuns, agreed to watch Elisabeth for a few hours, while I worked. When I returned, I could tell that they were exhausted and quite pleased that I was there to take her home. They talked about taking turns walking around with her, trying to get her to stop crying. I think the whole experience reinforced their commitment to celibacy.

Even though our days seemed so lethargically slow, the years passed by quickly. We celebrated our five-year anniversary with a small mass. We invited the people who had really companioned us during the difficult times, which truly was the entire five years. With tears in our eyes, Michael and I shared our vows again. "I, Mary, take you Michael to be my lawful husband, to have and to hold, from this day forward. For better or for worse, for richer or poorer, in sickness and in health." At that point I looked at Michael, and we started laughing.

"I get that now," I said, "To death do us part. I do."

We had a small reception at our house. The next day we took the kids to a friend's house, and Michael and I got on the road. We were going to go camping in a state park close by. Once we arrived, Michael started to drive to the more rugged area.

"Wait a minute," I screamed. "I need to be by the bathrooms. There is no way I am camping in the middle of nowhere."

"Mary," he said in a stern voice. "I didn't know this about you." I laughed because when we were younger, my family camped across the country and before we decided what campground we wanted to stay in, we had to first check out the bathrooms. If they weren't clean, we moved on to the next campground.

"I need to be close to a bathroom," I said again.

"I don't want to camp next to other people. I don't want them listening to my thoughts," he said.

My bubble of denial busted again as I realized his illness was traveling with us. Couldn't we have one weekend where his illness didn't take precedence? Reluctantly, Michael turned around and chose a site that was away from other campers but a close walk to the bathrooms. We made dinner, sat by the fire, talked and then went to bed.

The next morning, we realized that campers put up their tent fairly close to ours. "Let's go," Michael said. "I miss the kids." I knew he missed the kids (because I did too) but I really knew that he couldn't tolerate being close to other people. We packed up our gear and headed to town for breakfast. As we pulled into the parking lot of a restaurant Michael said, "I can't go inside. There are too many people in there. Do you mind if you order carry-out?" I breathed the heaviness of disappointment, knowing that this is not the way I wanted our anniversary weekend to go. I also knew it wasn't his fault, so I went inside and ordered a meal and then ate it in the car as we drove back in silence.

A few years passed, with ups and downs and yet another job change. I was getting used to the instability of our lives and tried to focus my energy on the kids. Leo had just gone through kindergarten and was going to enter first grade at the local elementary school. Lucy was about to go to kindergarten, and she was assigned to have the same wonderful teacher that Leo had. I had told the teacher a little bit about what was happening in our lives, and she was very supportive of us. Elisabeth was still in preschool so I had three kids in three different schools with three different schedules, adding to the craziness of our lives. I felt like I was a hamster on a wheel that went around and around and around — never slowing down or allowing me to get off. The wheel went so fast that often the littlest details fell through the cracks.

One day I was taking Lucy to her school and as we approached the parking lot, Lucy shouts, "Wow, there are no yellow buses." I looked around and said, "You're right, honey." Then I glanced at the sign that read: "No school today due to conferences." I must have missed that memo and a few others. "How lucky are we to have a day to ourselves to go on an adventure." Creating spontaneous "adventures" became my mantra throughout the years to come.

Keeping up with everyone's schedule in addition to T-ball, soccer practice and ballet almost did me in. I didn't know if I was coming or going. To add to the stress, I knew deep down that it was time that I brought more money in so that it would reduce some of the financial stress we were going through, and it would be a safety net just in case Michael lost his job or quit unexpectedly.

I had always talked about starting my own life coaching practice. I knew that I could coach out of my home or in an office and design my schedule according to the kids' needs. I had researched what I needed to do to start my own practice and I located a school in Nevada where I could learn the skills and then be certified. I applied online and then received a call the next day from the admission's coordinator. She asked about my educational and work background and my desire to be a coach. I spoke about how my passion was to work with women in midlife. I told her that when I was in graduate school, I was supposed to counsel college students but instead I formed a group for women in midlife. Each woman had recently experienced a major personal change, and yearned to figure out who they were and identify their true purpose.

At the end of our conversation, she invited me to the next training in Las Vegas, which was in two months. I was thrilled beyond words. I could barely contain my excitement. This was something just for me and just talking with her ignited my enthusiasm for midlife issues, women's development and the chance to companion people on their journeys. I was giggling with the thought that I would go out west, stay in a hotel by myself and get away from all the craziness at home. I desperately needed a break and I needed something that was just mine. I called Michael to see what he thought, and much to my delight, he agreed that it would be a good idea. I think I caught him in a good mood or he was going into mania because he didn't hesitate. I suggested that we invite his parents down to help him while I was gone, and he agreed.

Two months went by quickly, and Michael started to get sick again. He withdrew within himself and ignored the kids. I questioned whether I should go or not but I was determined to get this certification to help our family, and I knew that his parents would come down to help. I prayed that he could hold it together just a bit longer so I could go to Las Vegas and come back and start my business.

The day I left, I was excited and nervous. I wanted so badly to go but at the same time, I didn't know what would happen with Michael and his unpredictable behavior. By the time I boarded the plane I felt tremendous guilt, leaving Michael and the kids. We flew to Chicago and then had a three-hour layover. I went and grabbed something to eat. This is the longest I had been away from the kids since they were born. It was exhilarating to say the least. I sat in the food court and people-watched while I ate. I didn't have to share my French fries with anyone; they were all mine. I could go to the bathroom without changing a diaper or trying to contain toddlers in the bathroom stall. It was amazing. I felt like I did before I got married and had children, an independent woman with a huge heart for books, research and intellectual conversations.

We landed in Las Vegas while my luggage decided to go to California. My luck. I took a shuttle to the hotel, checked in at the front desk and waited for my luggage to arrive. The hotel was breathtaking as I walked into the sliding glass doors of the lobby. The floor was white marble patterned with black triangles and above the registration desk was a glistering gold chandelier sprinkling flakes of light around the room. I was enchanted with the luminous decorating and felt quite the wealthy woman, even though I wasn't. For a minute, I forgot about all that I left behind. I took the elevator to the second floor and followed the gold, red and blue tapestry carpet to my room. I swiped my card and slowly opened the door. The room was spectacular as it had six French doors that looked out into the beautiful painted-desert. I couldn't believe that I was there. I opened the doors, walked out onto the balcony and breathed in the dry air. It was such a beautiful sight. I stood there for what seemed like eternity, frozen in time and delighted by the beauty.

Walking around the resort was heavenly as well and with each step, I could feel myself decompressing. After a healthy meal at poolside, I went back to the room.

I knew it was time to call Michael and tell him that I arrived safely. I didn't want him to worry so I called home and waited as it rang over and over again. He didn't pick up the phone. Maybe his parents took them out for dinner or ice cream, or they got caught up in the bedtime routines. I left a message telling them that I loved them, and I would call tomorrow.

"Your luggage is here," I heard a voice outside the door say. I opened the door and while shoving some money in the bellboy's hand, I brought my suitcase inside and placed it on one of the queen-size beds. I was excited by this new opportunity but exhausted form the travels. I crawled into bed and slept like a baby that night.

Morning came very soon as I anxiously walked over to the room where the training was. There were 12 of us from all over the country being trained. Each woman shared their own story and together we bantered about coaching strategies, ideas on how to start our own business and ways to get our first client. It was intellectually stimulating, and I loved every minute of it.

The night before I was heading home, I received a call from Michael's mother saying that Michael had demanded that they go home. "Did he look like he was struggling?" I asked.

"Well, yes in a way. The weird thing is that he demanded that we go home. I didn't want to but he said that he was fine on his own."

"Do you think I need to get a flight back now?" I asked.

"No. I think he will be all right until you return tomorrow morning. We will keep calling to check up on him."

"Thank you so much. I will call a few friends, too, and ask them to stop by as well."

I felt sick to my stomach as I hung up, filled with guilt for leaving them and fearing that something bad would happen to the kids. When Michael was manic, he wasn't able to keep an eye on the kids, and I knew that three young kids were difficult to manage even if you didn't have a mental illness.

Our non-stop flight seemed to take longer as I kept checking my watch and looking at my phone. I wanted to be there and every second in the air made me more and more anxious. Finally, we landed in Detroit and I headed to the long-term parking lot. I got in my car and drove quickly home. I pulled in the driveway and took out my luggage and headed inside. It was quiet — too quiet. I placed my luggage in the kitchen and headed to the stairs to see where everyone was.

"Michael? Where are you?" I called. I could hear Lucy and Elisabeth upstairs. I walked over and looked up. There at the top of the stairs stood Lucy and Elisabeth. They were banging on the guest room door with tears in their eyes. I ran upstairs and gave them a big hug asking what they were doing. Daddy and Leo are in there, and they won't let us in. I could hear the loud music being played but that was about all. It gave me a chill knowing that the kids were outside of the room and couldn't get in. I banged on the door.

"Michael. Open the door now." After a few minutes, I could hear him walk to the door and unlock it.

"Why didn't you let Lucy and Elisabeth in? Didn't you hear them knocking? What is wrong with you that you would lock them out of the room?"

"Oh, don't start anything Mary. I have been with the kids all weekend. They were fine out there until you came home."

I went and picked up Leo and gathered the other two leaving Michael alone in the room. We went down the stairs, and I distracted them with "Let's see what I brought home for you." We ran into the kitchen, opened the suitcase and I brought out three stuffed animals. The kids were thrilled as they ran into the living room to play with their new toys.

Michael came down the stairs and walked right past me. "What happened to your mom and dad?" I asked. He said nothing, walked out the back door, and I could hear the ignition of the car as he drove down the long driveway. I fed the kids lunch and later dinner and then put them to bed. Michael still wasn't home but it was peaceful without him. In the wee hours of the morning, Michael came in the bedroom, quietly got under the covers and fell asleep. He didn't say anything. The next day Michael went to work and I went back to our routine.

When I was at the coach-training program, the instructors

challenged us to start our practice by getting one client the first week we were back. I thought that it was impossible due to the Michael's illness and instability. The first Friday after I came back from the training, the kids and I went to a surprise birthday party for a dear friend of ours. I chatted with others while watching the kids run circles in the open room. I met a woman who shared that she was struggling with what she wanted to do in life. She had said that she had tried therapy but didn't feel that she was getting anywhere. I told her about coaching. She was intrigued and asked if she could start working with me. I was so excited to say yes and to start my practice.

As I WAS TRYING TO keep up with the kids and their school, sports schedules and my new coaching practice, which I wasn't doing very well, Michael was in his own world. Even though I had dinner made every night, he said that he wasn't hungry, and he was trying to fast for religious purposes. I asked him to elaborate on that but he shrugged his shoulders and said that he just wanted to go into the office and read. I wanted to believe that he was on a fast as we knew many faith-filled people did, but I knew deep down it was more than that. At first he lost a few pounds and then it was 20. As he dropped weight, he began to look like a skeleton of who he was. It was as if the man I loved was disappearing right before my eyes. I tried making his favorite foods, baked desserts and stocked up on his favorite ice cream but he refused to eat.

I began questioning whether the cost of his instability was too much for the kids and me. I thought about leaving on many occasions but the unknown seemed more frightening than the safety in knowing what to expect.

We had made plans to go away for a weekend. We rented a cabin in a beautiful state park nearby. We had to reserve it a year in advance because it was a popular family destination so as each month passed, we were more eager to go. The kids were excited to explore the woods. As the weekend quickly approached, I began to dread spending time with Michael. The months leading up to this long-awaited date were tense. Seeing him so thin and hearing him talk about living in castles made me so depressed. His odd and erratic behavior burst my bubble of denial leaving me standing in grief and despair. As we were driving to the state park, I could tell he was manic. He was talking so fast it was hard to keep up with him. His words were like one big run on sentence with no breaths in between. He talked about learning to speak German, living in a castle and the importance of fasting and praying to be a "good Catholic." I gave up trying to make sense of it. I just let him ramble as I drove to the cabin.

As soon as we pulled up to the cabin, the kids were restless to explore. Struggling to get out of their car seats on their own, I unbuckled each one and with boundless energy they ran to the front door of the cabin without noticing the swarming of cicadas.

They were all over, the cicadas. They were camouflaged in the trees, clinging desperately to the bushes, clutching for dear life onto the screens and stuck to the side of the cabin as if they were blobs of already chewed chewing gum. They tried fiercely to attach onto our clothing. As we made our way from the car to the cabin, I could hear the crunching of their shell-like bodies. In contrast, the loud piercing sound of their buzzing made me think that they were manic, too, and it also reminded me of the movie about a small town in Northern California that was besieged by vicious birds. It left me with an uneasy feeling (as if I didn't feel uneasy anyway). It was also kind of ironic that cicadas lie dormant underneath the ground for 17 years before they wake up and find their way out. Michael's illness was uncannily similar. It lay dormant until one day it comes out and shakes our world with the uproarious sound and manic unpredictable behavior.

Michael became more agitated as he walked nervously around the inside of the cabin, opening and shutting doors. He peered into each closet as if someone were hiding there. When he was satisfied, he moved on to the next closet. Open and shut, open and shut is what I heard coming from downstairs. I knew what he was doing but I tried to stay focused on the kids. After I unpacked the groceries, Michael recommended that we take a walk. Maybe if he hiked, he would get his energy out and calm down; at least that is what I hoped. Right behind our cabin was a beautiful wooded, winding trail that ran next to a small creek. The cicadas seemed to soak up the serene setting as if it were a fine wine. They were quiet and more sedated in their flight plans. The kids stomped their feet in the creek and giggled as they watched the water splash one another. After a few minutes, they each carefully selected a rock and threw it in the creek, anticipating the ever-expanding ripple. Meanwhile, Michael was getting restless as he tugged on my arm.

"Mary. We need to talk. I think we want different things. What do you want in our marriage?"

I kept one eye on the kids and the other on the path ahead. "Well, I want to live where we do, close to my Mom, watch our kids grow up and excel in our careers. What do you want, Michael?"

"I want to live in a castle."

"A castle?" By this point, my anger reached a boiling point as I reflected on all the sacrifices I had to make in order to keep our lives halfway stable. Moving to me was not an option. Didn't he see how crazy this sounded?

"Michael, all I want is for you to be well and for our marriage to be happy. I want you to hold down a job for a few years. You don't understand how hard this has been and tough your illness is on our family. Your illness is our reality. And plus, I don't think you are well right now."

"Mary, stop blaming my illness. I am doing better than ever, and you know that you are having issues with our marriage. It is not my illness; it is you. You are not used to me doing well. So stop saying that I am sick."

"Okay, Michael."

I was pretty mad at this point but tried not to show it.

63

"Here is what I want," I said adamantly. "I want the kids to be safe and happy. I want to stay here. My Mom is here. Michael, please let our lives be stable for just a few years. I beg you. We have been through too much, and I can't handle any more changes. It has been way too much."

"I think we are going in different directions, Mary," he said in a monotone voice.

With that, I glanced ahead. There was a fork in the trail with two paths, one heading to the right and the other heading to the left. And in an instant, I had a deep, deep sense of knowing, undeniable knowing that I was going to be walking down one trail with the kids and Michael was going down the other, never to meet again. I realized I could no longer do this anymore, and I needed to part ways and get a divorce. I didn't believe in divorce nor did I ever think I would be divorced but there was peace in knowing that the kids and I didn't have to live under such torrential stress any longer.

While he kept talking about living in a castle, I started to think about all that I needed to do prior to asking for a divorce. I needed to stockpile supplies such as diapers, paper towels, canned goods and toilet paper. After all, Michael was the main source of income and I needed to make it for a while on my contract work until I knew the kids were alright and I could go back to work full time. My mind was running wild literally thinking about the enormity of this next step.

We gathered the kids and walked the rest of the way back to the cabin. I started to make dinner while the kids played in the family room. Michael insisted on not having the television on, and I knew that he was paranoid. He thought that the TV was speaking to him. The kids played with toy cars and Barbie dolls while I set the table. We were all pretty tired and hungry at this point, so conversation was minimal. After dinner, I bathed the kids and put on their cotton pajamas and tucked them into bed. Sitting on the floor next to their beds, I sang their favorite hymn. Quickly, they fell fast asleep. They looked so innocent. It hurt my soul to know that my next decision would change their lives forever.

Michael and I were exhausted from the day. He took a sleeping pill and quickly fell asleep on the couch. I placed a quilt over him and gently slid a pillow under his head. I then lay down next to him, and snuggled up like we usually did at night. With tears in my eyes I looked at my sleeping husband. I knew that this would be the last time we would go on a vacation together as a family.

I remembered all the times we went to the ocean to get away. We sipped coffee in a small coffeehouse as the kids used red, green and blue crayons to draw pictures on the back of the placemats. As a family, we took train rides, walked in the woods and played on the local playgrounds. Somehow when we were away, Michael was more relaxed and his symptoms were less obvious. I was always so happy on those vacations. He was the man I fell in love with, who made me laugh so hard until I cried, who loved and supported me through the labor and delivery of our three children. How could this be happening? We had many good times, but the tough times definitely outweighed the good. And then I thought about my list, adding to it as I fell asleep. Sippy cups. Winter clothes, boots… and I drifted off to sleep. When we woke up, I was anxious to pack the car so that we could go home, and I could start planning the next step.

As soon as we were home, I went shopping and started to stockpile supplies in the basement so that Michael wouldn't think anything was wrong. I bought juice boxes, microwavable mac and cheese and stashed cans of fruit and vegetables in plastic boxes on the shelves.

For some reason, I bought 12 cans of green beans. We didn't even like green beans. I hid them all behind the big artificial Christmas trees. I draped packages of toilet paper and paper towels with sheets so they were hidden from sight. Checking off my list, I bought a little at a time so it would not look suspicious.

Michael was still going at a rapid speed in his mind and in his behaviors. He would run on a track at a super-fast speed or mowed the lawn at a quick, flash-of-light pace. I often wondered what the neighbors thought when looking out their windows.

One late afternoon as we were playing games on the kitchen table, Michael looked at me and asked, "Are you having an affair?"

I quickly scooted the kids into the other room and put on a video. I didn't want them to hear what was going on.

"Me? An affair? You have got to be kidding. Why would you say that?"

"I think you are having an affair."

"Well I am not," I insisted. "How in the hell would I have time to have an affair while taking care of our kids and you?" I was fed up so I changed the subject by suggesting that we get out of the house and get something to eat. He said he didn't want to go and Leo said the same. I then took Lucy and Elisabeth out to a nearby restaurant while Michael and Leo stayed at home — at least that is what I thought. When we got home, I noticed that his car was gone.

I started our bedtime routine and put the other two to bed. I kept glancing at my watch wondering when they were going to come home. It was dark outside and way past Leo's bedtime. I couldn't imagine where they were and I was getting worried. I kept calling Michael's cell phone but it just went to voicemail. "Michael, it is late. Please come home. Leo needs to go to bed." He never called back. I frantically called my in-laws and they said that they hadn't heard from him. They assured me that everything was going to be okay and most likely they were just having fun and didn't check the time. I knew that they didn't have a clue how sick their son was.

As minutes turned into hours, I was getting more anxious. I called Don, one of his friends from college, and told him about Michael's odd behaviors and how he was reading the Bible obsessively and fasting. Don said, "Mary, good Catholics fast. He probably just went out for a short drive with Leo. He will be back." "This is not about being a good Catholic," taking his comment as an insult to my faith. "There is something wrong and I know it. If you hear from him, will you please call me right away?"

"I don't think you have anything to worry about, Mary." He didn't get it. He didn't understand how sick Michael was either. Frustrated I hung up the phone without saying goodbye.

His response made sense to me though because earlier Michael had convinced his parents, family and even his therapist that we were having marital problems and that I was saying that he was sick because I wasn't used to him being well. The sad thing is that Michael, even in his illness, presented so well that many people believed him. They didn't live with him to see how odd his behavior was and to see all that led up to an episode. They only heard his voice over the phone and he could sound normal for short periods of time. And all of his conversations were short.

I felt I kept shouting that something was wrong but no one heard me nor took me seriously. They talked to me as if I was exaggerating and making a big deal out of nothing. I felt like I was buried alive, screaming at the top of my lungs yet no one heard me.

Finally, at midnight, I heard the car pull into the driveway. Michael and Leo got out of the car and Leo came running toward me. "Mom, look at the pictures I drew." He showed me copies of pink, blue and orange paper with nothing on it except one, a crayon drawing he made and copied. Without even an explanation of where they had been or an apology for keeping Leo up late, Michael walked away past me, ignoring my words. He walked downstairs in the basement.

Trying to not upset Leo, I looked again at the copies and said, "I have never seen better copies than these. Good job. Now let's get ready for bed! Do you want a snack? Are you hungry?" As I poured a glass of milk for Leo I could hear Michael moving things around in the basement. I was afraid he would stumble upon the supplies I had tucked away. Within a few minutes, he brought up the red tent that we got from my aunt and uncle for our wedding.

"Let's sleep in the tent tonight," Michael said to Leo, still ignoring that I was standing there. Leo was excited at the mere thought of spending more time with his dad so he ran outside with Michael anxious to help him pitch the tent. Trying to be quiet as to not wake the neighbors, I said, "Michael, I am getting Leo a snack and after that, I am going to get him ready for bed. It is late, and he needs to sleep in his own bed. It is also starting to rain and I don't want him to catch a cold." He ignored my plea.

"Please come in, Michael," I begged him. "It's too chilly out here. Let him sleep in his own bed and maybe in a few weeks you can camp in the backyard. Please, Michael. Come in now."

"No!" he said in a loud, angry voice.

I retreated inside and stood at the back door as they put the tent up, crawled inside and zippered up the canvas door. I waited there for two hours and then went into my room and lay down on my bed. I dozed off to sleep until I heard the back door opening. I thought he was finally bringing Leo back in the house and into his room. Relieved I went back to sleeping hoping that all would be right until the morning. We could deal with it then. It was too late to have a discussion, and I was exhausted beyond words. I could hear Michael's footsteps as he came down the stairs. He quietly came into our bedroom and kissed me on the cheek and whispered, "I love you very much." I was so tired and so mad at him, I didn't say anything. I just pretended that I was asleep.

I fell asleep until I heard the slamming of the back door. I heard the car door shut and the ignition turned on. I jumped out of bed to see what was going on, and I ran out to the driveway. It was a cool, misty June night. The moon shed light on the wet driveway, and I could see the tire tracks on the black pavement. I ran to the tent, yanking the red canvas open. Leo wasn't there. I darted upstairs to his room. He wasn't there either.

Pulling his pillow to my chest while grasping onto his baby blanket, the one my mother made for him, I took a deep breath trying to smell his scent while looking around the room. Was he under the bed? Was he in the closet? He wasn't anywhere. He was gone. I ran down the stairs and went into Lucy and Elisabeth's room. I thought maybe that he crawled into bed with one of them. He wasn't there. I then ran out the back door to the driveway, where Michael's car was parked. It was gone. Leo was gone.

My knees collapsed from underneath me as tears streamed uncontrollably down my cheeks. Wailing a deep, raw sound of unmistakable woundedness, I screamed, *"WHERE IS MY BABY? WHERE IS MY BABY? MICHAEL, WHAT DID YOU DO WITH MY BABY? BRING HIM BACK. PLEASE MICHAEL BRING HIM BACK TO ME. BRING BACK MY BABY."* And then I could scream no more. It was as if a wrecking ball pounded into me, knocking me to the ground, taking my breath away and shattering my heart in a million tiny pieces. I placed my hands on the wet pavement, touching the tire tracks and sobbing.

RAIN WAS BEGINNING TO CLOAK me in heaviness as I struggled to stand up. I stumbled into the house. I felt void of all emotion, as I went to the front door and stared at the long, dark street for any signs of headlights on the black asphalt. After what seemed like an hour, I went into the kitchen and picked up the paper that Leo had given me hours before. It was one of the pictures that he had drawn and made copies of. I taped it to the door. When Leo came back home, I wanted him to see it and know that we were waiting for him. It was as if that picture represented a lit candle in the window or a yellow ribbon on a tree announcing that someone was missing. I stood there and listened to the tick of our clock….2:00…2:01….2:02…2:03…2:04….and then it was 5:00….5:01. The clock continued to tick, as I stood vigilant.

Night turned into day, as I remained standing by the door. Paralyzed with helplessness, I stood rigid like a guard. I could hear the quiet rumblings of Lucy and Elisabeth as they talked with one another and got out of bed. I greeted them at their door trying to make things as normal as possible. "Where's Leo?" Lucy asked in a sleepy tone of voice. "Honey, he is with daddy and they will be back later. Who wants to eat? How does oatmeal sound to you?" They ran into the kitchen and wiggled into their high chairs, eagerly waiting for their meal. It worked. They believed me, I thought to myself. They think this is a normal day.

A few hours passed, and I knew that Michael was not coming home. Sliding a movie into the DVD player, I placed bowls of cheese fish crackers in front of them hoping that they would not notice my exit from the room.

"911? I need to report a missing child," I whispered into the phone.

"Whose missing child?" the woman asked.

"My child. My son. My husband is mentally ill, and he took our six-year-old son last night and they haven't returned."

"Okay. Let me take down your address, and I will send an officer over there to take a report. That is the first step."

"Thank you."

I quietly walked to the front door watching the kids be captivated by their favorite video. A police car pulled into the driveway, and two officers in their uniforms got out of the patrol car and walked up the stairs to the front door. I ushered them into the kitchen and quietly said, "My husband is mentally ill. He has been acting very strange lately. I think he stopped taking his medicine. He was very angry, too, and left in the middle of the night with our six-year-old son. I have tried calling but it just goes directly into voicemail. Please help me."

"Ma'am did you say that you are still married? Is he still your husband?"

"Yes, I did but I am planning to file within the next few weeks. I had to get everything in order before I told him I wanted a divorce because I didn't know how he would react."

"But right now, you have no separation agreement or divorce papers."

"No. I don't."

"Ok, let me get this straight, he is the father of your son, and you have had no previous 911 emergency calls or no prior domestic violence charges."

"No. But I know he is sick, and I know he can't take care of Leo, our son, right now. He is so mentally ill, and he is belligerent as well. I am afraid of what he might do or where he might go."

"I understand that but it is too early to file a missing child report. Call us in the evening if he hasn't returned and then we will file a formal report."

"What happens if he doesn't come back? He could be on the road for a long time, and we will never find my son. I heard that the first 24 hours are the most critical in finding a missing child. Anything could happen — please file a report now."

"We can't do that, but call us later if he does not return."

"Should I call his cell phone and say if he does not bring Leo back, then I will call the police?"

"You can do that, but let me try calling instead." I was ambivalent about his calling because I didn't know if it would scare Michael and make him madder. Based on his first episode, at that time, he felt compelled to get in a car and just drive. I prayed that that was a one-time thing like the psychiatrist said.

I waited patiently trying to listen in on the call. I heard the dial tone; then Michael's voicemail message and then a beep. "Mr. Sullivan, this is officer Bob. I need you to come home now and bring your son. Nothing will happen if you come home now." He hung up the phone, and he and his partner looked at me as if they thought what they did was going to bring my baby home.

We all walked into the living room where the kids were. They looked up at the officers with their big eyes almost in awe that the police who are on the cartoons were actually in our home. I introduce the men to my kids, and the officers gave them each a plastic police badge. Lucy asked, "Can I have another one for my brother? He's with daddy right now but they should be home soon, right, mom?" "Yes lovey," I said. The officer handed her a third one. They were both so excited, and they had no clue what was really happening. They just knew that Leo was with daddy, and the police came to say hello and give them badges.

Evening arrived and there was no sight of Michael or Leo. By this time, my heart was beating fast, and I could barely catch my breath. Where were they? Are they still driving? Did Leo wear his seatbelt? Is he cold? Is he scared? I dialed 911 and told the dispatcher that they hadn't returned. The woman answering the calls recognized my voice and said that she would send an officer over right away.

In the meantime, I got the kids ready for bed, putting their soft sleepers on and placing them in Michael's and my bed. I took a deep breath relieved that I had made it to the night and that the police could finally look into it. I sat on the bed and sang their favorite songs. They quietly sang along with me. Hearing their little voices gave me chills — especially knowing that one voice was missing.

Almost as soon as they closed their eyes, there was a faint knock on the door. I opened it and saw the two police officers standing there. I whispered that the kids were sleeping, and I didn't want to wake them up or alarm them. We went into the kitchen. With their clipboard in hand, they asked the questions of how long we were married, if there was any drugs involved, if there was any domestic violence in our relationship, if Michael had said anything about taking a trip or if he had packed any clothes. I told them that we were married eight years and that both of us never used drugs nor did he ever lay a hand on me. I confessed we drank wine every once in a while, but that was the extent of our happy hour. I also told them that they left with the clothes on their back. He didn't pack anything for himself or Leo. Officer Bob took detailed notes as I spoke about the sequence of events.

As they were leaving, he said that a detective would be assigned to the case in the morning and someone should be giving me a call. I thanked them even though I was so irritated that we had to wait to file a report and that we were not able to have an Amber Alert. I quietly shut the door and sat down on the couch, emotionally and physically exhausted as if someone squeezed the last piece of energy out of my tired body.

Morning came, painting the sky with pink rays of the sunrise. It was beautiful and for a second, I forgot what had happened. Then reality hit. I started to think about the conversation with Officer Bob and the more I thought, the more infuriated I became that they didn't file a report earlier. Did they think I was lying about it? Why did they give Michael the benefit of the doubt? I knew him, and I knew he was sick, very sick. I thought about waiting for the detective to call but then I questioned, "Why wait?" No one would fight harder to find Leo than me. I was tired of feeling helpless and waiting around for other people to take action. He was my son, and I needed to take things in my own hands.

I SAT DOWN AT THE KITCHEN table and made a list of people I thought could help. I needed people with different skills than me so that we could look at every aspect of this impending search. I always joked about just having a right-brain and no left-brain, but I realized that I was more creative than logical, and I needed a team that would balance me out.

The first person I called was my best friend from college, Millie. She always knew what I was thinking and could finish my sentences. Meredith was next on my list because she always knew the right thing to say. I knew that I needed my mom who would help me with the kids, and I needed Eli who was a logical thinker and who could help with the details of the search. The only one I lacked was someone to organize the information. With that thought, the phone rang. It was my friend Karen from church.

"Mary, John and I just got off a flight and I can't stop thinking of you. Are you okay?"

"Karen, Michael is very sick. He took Leo last night, and we don't know where they are."

"Oh my God." And then there was a pause. "Okay. Let me stop by my house and check on my kids and then I will be over."

I immediately started calling the rest of the people on my list. Some I could get in touch with and others I left a message. "Michael took Leo, and we don't know where they are. The police are involved, but I want to start my own search. If you can help me find him, the door is open. Please help me."

One by one they came to the door ready to help, bringing bagels, coffee and sweets to the house. I couldn't fathom eating but I knew that the rest of the group would get hungry. The most difficult call to make was to my mom.

"Mom. Michael took Leo."

"What do you mean, he took Leo?"

"Mom. Michael is very sick right now. He is not himself, and he took Leo. We don't know where they are. The police are involved. Mom, I need you."

"Mary, I will be right over. I love you."

"I love you too, Mom."

It was noon before everyone arrived. We gathered around the long wooden farm table in our kitchen. It was the same table that Michael and I bought after we found out that we were pregnant with Leo. We wanted a long table in order to accommodate our growing family. It was at this table where we held hands and said our prayers before each meal. At Easter, we gathered at the table to dye eggs, spilling splotches of pink, yellow and green stain on the dark wood. There were chips and gouges from meals gone wild with tiny fists flying in the air holding silverware and banging it relentlessly on the table, while refusing to eat one more bite. There were birthdays, baptisms, holidays and pumpkin carving contests, not to mention all the art projects that drastically went wrong — all at that same table.

We sat there and began to brainstorm different ways we could find them. Meredith suggested that I call the credit card companies to see if he made any charges. We had a few joint accounts but I knew that Michael opened a few more in the past month. He said it was for his business but I couldn't recall how many he had. I looked through his files for a folder that listed the cards, and I found it. I first called the companies of the cards that were under both of our names. There were no recent purchases. I then called a credit card that was in his name.

"Please help me," I pleaded. "My name is Mary Sullivan and my husband suffers from bipolar disorder, and he is having a psychotic episode. He abducted our six-year-old son in the middle of the night and I don't know where they are. Please this is my baby, you have to help me find them."

"Well, Ms. Sullivan, I can't give you that information since it is in his name."

"Do you have a child?" I asked.

"Yes, I do. I have four."

"So you know how much you love your child and what if someone took one of them, and you didn't know where he was?"

With a heavy sigh, she said, "That is my greatest fear — any mother's worst nightmare. Okay. Let me look at it. You know, I am not supposed to do this but I do see a charge at a pizza restaurant. And then there is a gas charge and wait a minute... it looks like there are plane tickets purchased with this card at the Detroit airport. Plane tickets. That is all I see right now."

"Oh my God. What has he done?" I took a deep breath and then said "Thank you. Thank you so very much."

"He has plane reservations out of the Detroit airport. It looks like they are going to New York."

Right away Millie was dialing the airport and asking to speak to someone from the airlines with a flight to New York. After a few minutes and many transfers, someone picked up the phone. "How can I help you?"

"I need to know if a man and a little six-year-old boy made the flight to New York. I could hear her breathe a sigh of relief and said "Thank God. They didn't make their flight."

I called the credit card company again and spoke to the same woman who answered my first call. "I have been thinking about you, and I found another purchase. It looks like they rented a car at the airport." By the time I hung up the phone Eli was calling the car rental place. He handed the phone to me.

"Can I help you?"

"Yes. I need your help desperately. Did a young man and a six-year-old boy just rent a car there?"

"Yes. They did. They just left the lot. The man said that they were heading to New York City to catch a flight out of LaGuardia airport. The man looked nervous. He was pacing back and forth as if he was in a hurry. The little boy looked tired. Why?"

"That little boy is my son, and my husband is mentally ill. He took our son in the middle of the night."

All of a sudden more dots were being connected as I realized there were many international flights leaving that airport. It all made sense now. Michael was taking classes to learn how to speak German. He actually met with a tutor to help him. He never told me this but I found the sessions scheduled on his calendar and the payment in our checkbook. And there was a lot of talk about a castle in Germany. Oh my God. He is going overseas with Leo. How will I ever find them now? I heard a story about a husband who abducted his son and went to a foreign country. It took years for the woman to find them.

One step at a time Mary. We only need to take one step at a time, I reminded myself. Millie began dialing the phone to the airport. When someone answered, she handed the phone to me.

"Do you have a passenger named Michael Sullivan who I think is getting on a flight to Germany with a six-year-old boy?"

I could hear her typing on the computer and then she said, "Yes. We have him, and he is traveling with a young boy. They were supposed to arrive on a flight from Detroit and switch planes and head to Frankfurt, Germany. Let me check." There was a long pause, "Let's see. It looks like they didn't make the flight because they didn't have a passport for the boy."

"Thank God. The man is my mentally ill husband, and that boy is my precious son, who he took in the middle of the night.

Thank you so much for helping me. Do you know where they were headed?"

"No. I just saw them walking away. I didn't speak to them but my colleague did. Let me ask her." There was a pause and then she got back on the phone and said, "No. He didn't say where he was going or if he was going to take a different flight. I am so sorry we couldn't give you more information."

"That's okay," I said. "I really appreciate your help. If we don't hear from him soon, I think I will just head to New York. Do you have any tips for me on how to navigate such a large airport and city? I haven't been there since I was a kid and that was a long time ago."

"When you get here, ask for a yellow cab."

Without questioning, I said, "I will. Thank you again."

When I hung up the phone, I heard Eli dialing the number to the car rental place who confirmed that Michael returned the car at the airport, and there were no other rentals.

"Alright, so they must be somewhere in New York City. Let's think about where they might go in New York."

"How are we going to find them in such a big city?" I asked.

"I know one step at a time."

Our neighbor, having heard of my predicament through the grapevine, knocked on the door and asked if she could take the kids to the zoo for the day. Relieved by the mere thought of not having to worry about them while focusing on the investigation, I said yes. While I was getting the backpack filled with wipes, snacks and juice boxes, the rest of the group were sitting at the table, brainstorming every possible angle to find Leo.

As I walked back into the kitchen after hugging Lucy and Elisabeth, I heard Millie say, "How about calling a detective? Do you think they would know something we don't?"

"Yes. It is worth a try. We don't want any stone left unturned," Eli said. "Millie, I will help you find the name of a local detective.

I have my laptop here." They went off to the other room to search different names.

Meredith chimed in, "Let's check with the detective who is assigned to the case. Let's update him on what we have found out so far." She tried calling the detective and had to leave a message.

It was mid-afternoon and while this entire flurry was happening in my kitchen, I heard my cell phone ring. We all stopped dead in our tracks with the sound. I slowly answered and said, "Hello?" I heard Michael's voice on the other end of the line. Kevin ran up and I tilted my head so he could hear.

"Where are you Michael? Is Leo there? Is he alright?"

"Mary. You put a hold on the credit cards. You need to release them now. I can't use them. I need money now. How dare you do this to your son and me? I demand you to call the banks and credit cards now. They won't listen to me. Now, Mary!"

"Michael. Where are you? Let me come and get you guys. I am so sorry that we argued. Please tell me where you are. Where are you, sweetheart?"

Eli was motioning me to keep him on the phone as long as I could so that we could track from where he was calling. And then I heard Leo's voice, "Can I talk to mommy?" Click. Michael hung up.

Eli picked up the phone and dialed the number again. It rang and rang and rang. He was able to trace the call. "They are still in New York, Manhattan. It looks like they called from a pay phone on 42nd Street. He will call back. Let's wait. He needs money. I know he will call back."

I knew it was time to call the detective myself and see if he returned to the office. I dialed the number still shaking from the call. A woman answered the phone. "Detective's office. Can I help you?"

"Yes. My husband abducted our six-year-old son and went to New York City. He called my cell phone, and we were able to trace it. They are in New York City."

"Mary, is that you?"

I hesitated and said, "Yes," confused as to whom I was talking with.

"Mary, this is Karen, remember me?"

I knew Karen from my old church. I used to provide spiritual meditation workshops and she sang a cappella. I always told her that she had a voice of an angel and the mere sound of her voice made me cry. "Karen," I said. "You still have the voice of an angel."

"Ah, Mary, I am so sorry this happened. We will find them. I have contacts in New York, and I will call them when we hang up and ask them to issue an Amber Alert in all five boroughs."

"Karen, I can't thank you enough."

"Where do you think they are?"

"Well, we traced them to 42nd street but Michael is very manic and when he is manic he walks extremely fast. I can't imagine Leo being able to keep up with him. I am so afraid that Michael will leave Leo somewhere or that someone will snatch him. Please, Karen, you have to help me."

"I will Mary," she assured me.

As soon as I hung up with Karen, the phone rang again, and it was Michael. "Michael, where are you?"

"I'm not telling you where we are. You need to send me money now!"

"Michael? Is there a local church that you can stop by the rectory and speak to a priest? He will probably give you a place to stay and something to eat until morning and Leo can rest his feet. You both must be so tired." Click, he hung up again.

I sat there in utter stillness, exhausted and drained. I went into my home office away from all of the activities. I sat in my grandfather's chair in my office, the one he gave me before he passed away. I plopped down on the chair, leant my head back and took my wedding rings off my finger and threw them with vengeance at the bookshelf in the corner.

It was around 5:00 in the early evening when the kids came

back. Mom, who stayed with me all day, made dinner for them and put them to bed in my room. I went in to sing our songs and kiss them goodnight.

"When is daddy and Leo going to be home?" Lucy asked.

"Soon, very soon," I replied. I sat there with them until they fell asleep. Tiptoeing out of the room, I shut the door just slightly so they wouldn't feel afraid. Light turned into darkness and one by one, everyone left to go to his or her own homes.

I hated when it was dark. I felt hopeless and terrified waiting for the sun to rise. The hours went by so slowly as I watched the clock. I hated the helplessness I felt knowing my son was gone and everyone else was sleeping as if nothing happened that day. They would wake up the next day and begin their weekend routine of soccer games and cookouts while I sat around waiting.

I sat in my grandfather's chair, and I began to pray to him and my deceased father. "Grandpa, dad, please help me find Leo. Please do whatever you can to keep him safe until he is in my arms again."

I then began to pray the rosary. "*Hail Mary, full of grace, the Lord is with thee. Blessed art thou amongst women, and blessed is the fruit of thy womb, Jesus. Holy Mary, Mother of God, pray for us sinners now and at the hour of our death. Amen.*" I paused and wondered if I prayed the rosary all night, would Michael and Leo come back home? If I just prayed a few decades of the rosary, will my prayers be heard? *What do I need to do to get my son back? Please Lord. Hear my prayers. I want him back safe in my arms. You gave him to me. Please don't take him away from me now. I love him so much. I love everything about him. Please, Lord. Help me. My heart is breaking, and I need your help desperately. Please, please give me back my Leo. I beg you.*"

Hours later, around midnight, I felt exhausted from crying and praying. I wanted the pain to go away. I wanted to wake from this horrid nightmare and realize it was just that...a terrible nightmare...and Michael would wake up, make breakfast, and I would wake up with the kids. Together we would gather around the table and eat pancakes. But I knew that it wasn't a nightmare. It was my reality.

I got up from the chair and headed to my bedroom where Lucy and Elisabeth were sleeping. They lay next to one another in their soft pastel-colored, footed pajamas. Elisabeth was sucking her thumb and holding tightly to her blanket that her godmother gave her, and Lucy was sleeping right next to her on the tall sleigh bed, the one that Michael and I bought before we got married. Do they even know what is going on? Do they know that their brother is missing? Do they understand? I slid in under the covers and gently moved them so that I could hold each one of them in my arms. I listened to their breath ... breathing in and out ... and I smelled the innocence of their freshly washed hair and their clean pajamas. I gently picked up Lucy's small hand and looked at each finger, taking in the beauty. Leo has the same fingers. I want my baby back! *Please God...I want my baby back.*

As I BEGAN TO CLOSE my eyes, I had a strong sense of intuition telling me that I would receive a call in the wee hours of the morning telling me that someone found Leo and that he was safe. It was a deep sense of knowing like the time I stood in the state park and saw the fork in the path. All I needed to do was to trust the process.

At exactly 1:30 in the morning, the phone rang. I awoke from a light slumber knowing that it was the call, the one I had been waiting for. I ran into the kitchen and grabbed the phone.

"Hello?"

"Ms. Sullivan, this is Marilyn. I am an EMT in New York City. We have your son, and we are taking him to the nearest hospital in Manhattan."

"You have my son? Is he okay? Please tell me that my baby is okay?"

"Ms. Sullivan, your son is alright. We found him sleeping under the Brooklyn Bridge. Two men were walking and saw him lying there. They called the police right away and stayed with your son until the EMT arrived."

"Is he okay?"

"Yes, he is okay, as far as we can tell, Ms. Sullivan. Once we get to the hospital, the nurse will check him out closer."

I started to weep uncontrollably. "Thank God, you have

my baby. Thank God, you have my baby and ... where was my husband?"

"Your husband, Ms. Sullivan, was found wandering down the street hunting through trash cans."

"He was what?" I asked in shock.

"He was down the street looking through trash cans."

"Oh my God, so Leo was alone? Anything could have happened," I said.

"Yes, it could have, but he is safe now. He is safe, Ms. Sullivan."

"Where is my husband now?" I asked, not really wanting to know.

"He has been arrested."

"Arrested?"

"Yes. He has been arrested and has been taken to jail. This is serious. Most likely he will be charged with child endangerment." After hearing that, I couldn't think about him anymore. I just wanted to hear my baby's voice. "Can I speak to my baby? Please, let me speak to Leo," I pleaded. "Yes, Ms. Sullivan, here is your son."

"Leo, this is mommy. I love you so much dear one. Are you alright?" I asked, trying hard to stay composed not wanting to scare him even more.

"Mommy? Mommy? I never want to come here again," he screamed in a shrill, trembling voice of terror that no mother wants to hear — the type of voice that takes your breath away and makes every cell in your body writhe in indescribable pain.

"I know, baby. I know, my sweet love. We won't go there again. I promise you. Listen to me carefully. These nice women are going to take you to the hospital to make sure you are alright. There will be good people there at the hospital to take care of you until I am there. When you wake up, little one ... when you wake up, you will be in my arms, and we will sing our favorite hymn. Remember our song?"

With my voice shaking, I began to sing, "Taste and see, taste and see." I heard his voice, "I remember, mommy."

"I love you so much, Leo."

"Love you too, mommy."

The EMT got back on the line and said, "I promise I will call you as soon as we arrive at the hospital. The doctor on call will check Leo for drugs."

"Drugs?" I hesitantly asked. "Why do you need to check him for drugs? He is too young!"

"No, Ms. Sullivan. We check all children who have been homeless."

"Homeless? My son is not homeless. He has a home."

"Oh, I know, Ms. Sullivan, it is just our policy to check all kids who have been on the streets."

I took in a deep breath, realizing that this was all so much bigger than me. I thanked her profusely for taking care of my precious son, and she assured me that they would keep him safe until I arrived in New York.

As soon as I hung up the phone, I called my sister. I knew that if I couldn't think coherently, she would, and she would help me get a flight.

"Anne. Michael is really sick, and he took Leo in the middle of the night, and the police just found them under the Brooklyn Bridge."

"Oh, my God, Mary. What do you need?" she asked.

"Is there any way you could get me a ticket to New York? I told Leo that I would be there when he wakes up. How in the hell am I going to do that, Anne? Good Lord, why did I even tell him that?"

"Mary. I will take care of it for you. Just be by your phone and start packing your bags." I hung up the phone relieved that I didn't have to figure that part out and that my sister would.

"Mary, are you okay?" I heard my mom's voice in the other room. I ran into the guest bedroom where she was lying down on the bed, and crawled in next to her as if I were a little girl afraid of the monsters under my bed.

"Mom, they found Leo under the Brooklyn Bridge. They found my baby. They really found him." I started to cry. She held me tight but I could still feel her body tremble.

"Was Michael with him?" she asked.

"Yes, but not really with him. The police found him walking down the sidewalk rummaging through trash cans... and Leo was sleeping on the sidewalk."

It was too much for both of us to fathom so she did what she always did best, "Lovey, everything will be alright. Leo will be in your arms soon. I can take care of the kids while you go to New York."

"Anne is making reservations for me so I am going to pack a bag and call Millie for a ride to the airport."

I ran upstairs into Leo's room and pulled out the third drawer of his dresser, the only drawer that had clothes in it. The other three drawers proudly protected his Batman costume and his Scooby-Doo bus and cars. Shorts, shirt, underwear and clean socks. I ran downstairs and into our bedroom and did the same for Michael. Shorts, shirt, underwear and clean socks. I threw them in a suitcase and put on clean clothes myself. I didn't have time to take a shower. I was anxiously waiting for Anne to call.

About 30 minutes later, after I called my sister, I heard my cell phone ringing, and it was Anne. "If you leave now, you can get a flight that takes off in one hour. Do you think you can do that? I will also book a flight and meet you at the hospital."

"Okay, I will meet you there as soon as I can."

"Thank you, Anne so much!"

I called Millie who picked up the phone right away and asked her if she could take me to the airport. About 10 minutes later, she drove up in her van with a cup of hot French vanilla coffee, steam still rising from the tiny hole in the plastic lid. We loaded my luggage in the back of her van and quickly got in the car. As we were backing out, she handed me a white envelope, which I could tell had money in it.

"You might need this — take it, please," she said.

"Millie, I can't take this."

I started to cry. I could no longer hold back the caged emotions from the past 48 hours. It wasn't a dainty cry, either; it was that ugly cry, the cry you don't even want your best of friends to see. I thanked her and stared blankly into the darkness.

She pulled outside the front of the airport and helped me with my luggage. There were only a few travelers walking the broad yet empty hallways. I checked in at the one counter that was opened, walked through security and then walked briskly and quietly to the gate. I never sat down because I was too nervous to sit. Instead, I paced back and forth and back and forth listening once again to the minute hand of the clock tick away. Where is everyone? I thought to myself. Don't they know that I need to get to the hospital to hold my son before he wakes? I wanted to scream at the top of my lungs, *"Let's get to work, everyone. This is serious. I need to get to my son."*

Finally, darkness turned into light as they called my flight. I stood in line anxious to board the plane. By then, more people gathered to line up. I had a seat by the window and the flight attendant handed me a pillow with a white, scratchy disposable case on it. I took it and placed it behind my head. I closed my eyes as we took off, but I couldn't sleep. I was thinking of all that I needed to do once I got off the plane like find a cab, get to the hospital and see Leo.

After a few hours we landed in New York. As soon as I got off the plane, I got caught up in the uncontrollable tight wave of people, weaving their way in and out of the aisles of the airport. When I saw the front doors, I quickly pulled away from the tight grips of the crowd and exited the airport. I saw that there was a line of travelers waiting for cabs. I stood in line and when it was my turn, I confidently repeated what the woman on the phone told me, "I need a yellow cab." The man looked at me with astonishment and said, "They are all yellow, lady." I looked at the cab in front, and it was yellow, so was the cab behind and the one behind that one. My God, I looked like an idiot. I must have lost my mind when I was talking to her. An attendant ran to me and handed me a handout listing the fees for different stops around the city. I must have looked so naive that he was afraid someone would take advantage of me.

"I need to go to the hospital as fast as you can, please." In a flash, we were on the roads dodging in and out of the lanes. Horns blaring and screeching tires kept my eyes wide open and my thoughts in prayer — of surviving the ride. I should have told him that I wanted to get there in one piece.

I glanced out the window and saw masses of men, women and children walking on the sidewalk like ants marching toward a desired piece of fruit. These people looked mindless listening to their tunes or talking on the phone unaware of others around them. A homeless mentally ill man stood facing an abandoned building and relieved himself on the rusty colored brick. The stench from garbage and the exhaust fumes filled the air. How could my baby be alive in this city?

We finally made our way to the hospital, barely missing the bike messenger by just a hair. The cab came to an abrupt, whiplash stop at the hospital's front entrance. I quickly opened the door while shoving money into the cab driver's hand not really caring how much I gave him. I just wanted out of the cab. I wanted to see my baby.

The hospital's sliding glass doors were dotted with greasy fingerprints. The moment I entered I was overwhelmed by the rancid smell of body odor. The waiting room was packed with people — young, old and many who looked like they had been sleeping on the streets for years. Some were sitting, others standing and quite a few were leaning on the walls, all waiting for their names to be called. "Johnson," I heard a nurse yell out into the waiting room. "Johnson. Is there anyone here named Johnson?" In the corner of the room, sat an old man looking through an outdated magazine. His straggly gray hair stuck out of a Yankee's baseball cap and his beard looked like it had food entangled in the strands. He slowly got up and shuffled toward the nurse.

"Yea, I'm Johnson. It is about time. I have been sitting here for over five hours waiting for you to call my name."

"Well, that I just did," said the nurse hurriedly directing him to the triage room. I glanced around the room trying to catch the eye of a staff member so that they could show me where my son was. But there was no one, except a police officer.

He was standing by a gray metal locked door that led to the ER treatment rooms. Dressed in a black uniform with his right hand placed on his gun, he glanced around the room. I ran up to him and screamed, "Please, let me in! My son is back there, and I need to see him now. Please, I beg you, I need to see my baby!" He looked surprised as I ran toward him but he seemed to listen to what I was saying. He picked up the phone and dialed a number. "There is woman who says that her son is back there. Do you have a kid there?" And then he paused. "Okay. I will let her in."

He pulled out a ring of clanging keys from his pocket and unlocked the door. I ran down the narrow, dingy hallway. It was as if everything was in black and white, and I was running in slow motion. I couldn't get back there fast enough. Turning a corner of the hallway, I stopped dead in my tracks. It was all becoming so real. Stretchers were lined up, and the curtains were open except for one: I knew my baby was behind that curtain. I ran past the doctor and nurses, stopped and then slowly pulled the curtain back. Laying in the long, hospital stretcher was my little boy. His body was so small compared to the long, narrow bed that he was laying on. His face was covered with splotches of dirt, his blond hair was dark and matted, and his clothes that I had recently purchased were filthy. His shoes were still on his feet, worn and scuffed.

Quietly walking to his side, careful not to wake him, I delicately lifted the white sheet that was covering his little body and looked at him sleeping. I picked up his hand. One, two, three, four, five — I counted his fingers just as I did when he was born. He was dirty from head to toe. I gently placed my trembling hands under his limp body. I picked him up and slowly cradled him in my arms. I pulled him close to my chest and deeply inhaled, taking in his smell, hearing the sound of his breath and feeling the weight of his little body in my arms.

Then I began to sing. It was the song I promised him that we would sing when I spoke to him on the phone in the ambulance — the song that we sang every night before he went to sleep. "Taste and see, taste and see," and with that he opened his swollen eyes and began to mouth the rest of the words, "...and see, taste and see." I stared into his blue eyes, afraid to close my eyes. I didn't want to take my eyes off him. How did he end up here, hundreds of miles away from home? How did my husband end up in jail? Why did this happen?

The police officer that was standing guard over Leo came over and whispered to me in his New York accent, "I have never seen a reunion like this. This is like a drama on TV." When did my life become a drama movie, I thought to myself.

"When you have a moment, I need to talk with you." I laid Leo back in his bed and walked over to where the officer was. "You need to know because of what your husband did, there is an open case with Jobs and Family Services."

"An open case?"

"Yes. I already talked to the caseworker and told them about your reunion. There is no doubt whatsoever that you are Leo's mom but they still need to talk to you." He gave me the number, and I used the phone next to the nurse's desk, still being able to keep my eye on Leo.

"Hello. My name is Mary Sullivan. I understand that you need to talk with me about my son, Leo."

"Yes. I spoke to the officer, and he seems assured that you are his mother. We will have an open case on your husband and when you get back to Michigan, there will be another open case with the department of family services there."

All of sudden, I was taken back by the enormity of the situation. For some odd reason, I thought I was going to pick Leo up and then bring Michael home to a hospital in Michigan. I didn't realize that they arrested him for child endangerment, and we would then have to go through the court process to get him out.

"Where is my husband?"

"Well, he is in a holding cell down at the jail. He will be there until he is arraigned."

"Can I go see him?"

"No. No one can go down there. You will see him at the arraignment."

"When will that be?" I asked.

"At midnight." Only in New York are there arraignments throughout the night. "Thank you," I said.

A nurse in her blue scrubs walked up to me as I hung up the phone. "I know that this is overwhelming for you so I called the social worker. She can help you with different resources in the city. Numbly, I went to Leo's bed, sat in the chair and held tightly on to his hand.

"Ms. Sullivan? I am Cheryl, and I am a social worker." She was a tall, thin woman in her forties with short, auburn hair and thick-rimmed glasses. Dressed in a navy blue skirt and a white blouse, she stood before me.

"I heard that you have experienced every mom's worst nightmare. I am so sorry for what you have been through but I am so glad that you found your son. It sounds like your husband is in jail awaiting his arraignment. Do you want to meet in the small room down the hall to discuss different resources that might be helpful to you?"

"Sure. If it is alright with you, I would like to wait until my sister comes so that she can wait with Leo. I don't want him to be afraid or think I left him. He has been through so much."

"No problem. I will be there. Just come in when you are ready."

I looked around the small area and noticed that there was a sink. The nurse brought over a small white washcloth, and I began to gently wash Leo's face, arms, hands and then the rest of the body, patting it dry with a towel. What initially was a white washcloth quickly turned brown due to the layers of soot, grime and dirt from being on the streets. I wanted to wash him clean of the experience, and I wanted to see the little boy that I knew, not the kid on the streets but my precious son.

It was now early afternoon and like a breath of fresh air, my sister came into the emergency room. With a white teddy bear in her arms and a bag of books, she hugged me. I tumbled in her arms, relieved that she was there. She then went over to Leo and gave him the bear. He held onto it and looked excitedly into her eyes. "I have some books that I thought we could read if you are up to it."

"Sure," Leo said.

"I will let you guys get to your reading while I talk to Cheryl down the hall. If you need anything I will be right down the hall. Okay, my love?"

Leo softly said, "Okay."

The room we were meeting in was small with the walls painted yellow. There was one beige rectangular table with a phone on it and two wooden chairs that creaked and wobbled when you sat down. "I guess what I need to do first is find an attorney for Michael."

"Here is a list of attorneys who represent mentally ill individuals who are caught up in the legal system. There is another list of mental health agencies that advocate for mentally ill criminals and see that they get a fair trial as well as the medication they need."

The word "criminal" caught me off guard. Oh my God. Michael is a criminal.

One by one, I called each number, told the person answering the phone my story and asked for guidance. One by one each person said they were unable to help me and so I checked them off the list.

After calling the last number, I wearily went back into the room where Leo was and slumped into the chair. My sister came up to me and said that she had talked to her husband who knew that name of a criminal attorney in town who was willing to speak to Michael. Feeling relieved yet depleted I asked, "Can you call him?"

"Sure," she said as she called on her cell phone. She walked out of the room, and I could hear the murmur of her conversation. She came back in and said that the attorney was heading over to the holding cell to see Michael.

"Whew," I said. The social worker walked into the room, and I walked over to where she was standing. "I think we have an attorney. My sister knows someone who practices in New York, and he said that he would go and talk to Michael right away."

"Okay. The next thing we need is a place for you to stay tonight. Most likely, Leo will be discharged in a few hours."

I reflected on the day. It seemed like it was never-ending. It started with getting the call in the wee hours of the morning, and then rushing to the airport before the sun came up. And now about 17 hours later, we are standing in the hospital waiting for Leo to be discharged and darkness again is upon us.

"Here is a list of hotels in the area but I know that there is a big convention here in the city and most likely it will be difficult to find a room and, if you did find one, it might be outrageously expensive."

My sister took the list and went into the small room. There were only a few rooms available in Manhattan, and, as predicted, they were going for an exorbitant price. Anne walked back to where we were and gave us an update. Cheryl, the social worker, was still with us.

"Wait a minute," she said. "There used to be an old convent above the hospital. When the nuns moved out, the hospital turned it into office space but there is still one room that is available for families who have loved ones in the hospital. Let me see if it is available."

ABOUT TEN MINUTES LATER, LEO had fallen back asleep, and Anne and I were whispering to one another, not wanting to wake him up. Cheryl came back. "Yes. The room is available. I have the key for you. When Leo is discharged, you can all stay in that apartment."

"How can I thank you enough?"

"It's no problem. This is what we are here for."

Leo was checked from head to toe before the discharge papers were signed. We placed the books my sister brought in the suitcase, and Leo held tightly onto his bear. We walked out of the hospital, walked down the sidewalk and opened a connecting door. There was a small lobby and an elevator on the right. Leo was excited to press the button and when he did, the doors immediately opened. "To the third floor," I said to Leo as his tiny finger pressed the round, lit button. "One, two and three floors. Here we are."

As we got off the elevator, we walked down a pale yellow narrow hallway with beige linoleum floors. There were offices on each side, and golden nameplates hung on each door. Our room was on the left. There was no nameplate. With my hands shaking, I fumbled in my purse and grabbed the key. Slowly I unlocked the door and entered the room.

Right across from the door was a small kitchen; just room enough for one person. Everything we could possible need was there: a small fridge, a stove, a microwave, plates and silverware and even a coffee maker with a bag of coffee sitting next to it. Down from the kitchen was the living room. There were two twin beds with dreary brown quilts on them and then under the window was a dark brown couch. We put our bags and suitcases down. Down the hallway was a bathroom with a pedestal sink and tiny black and white porcelain hex tile floors. It was sparkly clean and had thick white towels on the counter, like the ones you get in a fancy hotel. I was eager to get the all the dirt off Leo and let him play in the tub. I turned on the warm bathwater, checking the temperature with my finger, and helped Leo in the tub. I lathered the soap in my hands and allowed him to blow bubbles. He giggled, popping each one while I washed his hair.

After I dried him off and put clean pajamas on, my sister got a call. It was from the attorney. "Uh huh," she responded. "Let me let you talk to my sister." I went into the kitchen and took the phone.

"Mary, I spoke with Michael, and he said that he was going to fire me. He didn't want anyone that you or your sister hired because he does not trust you. He thinks you are working against him and want him to get in more trouble."

"He did that without me," I said.

"Mary, he is very sick and very paranoid right now. I can't do anything if he won't agree to it. I am sorry that I cannot help. When is his arraignment?"

"Midnight," I responded.

"Okay. I will call you tomorrow and see if there is anything I can do for you. In the meantime, the only alternative is legal aid. There are some good legal aid attorneys so hopefully you will be assigned to one of them soon. Don't hesitate to contact the attorney prior to the arraignment."

"I will," I replied. "Thank you so much for your time and kindness. I really appreciate it."

Anne went out to pick up a pizza and other groceries to bring back to the apartment while Leo and I set the small table for dinner. Except for snacking, we hadn't eaten the entire day, and we were ravished. When she returned, we ate in silence. We were starved. After dinner, I lay down with Leo and watched cartoons on the television. It was then 11 p.m. and I knew that I needed to head over to the courthouse for the arraignment. I didn't want to leave Leo but I felt that I needed to be there for Michael. After all, he was my husband — at least for now.

I hugged and kissed Leo goodbye and thanked Anne for being there. I walked outside. There was a heavy rain pounding down on the sidewalks soaking my entire body and leaving me with a cold chill. "To the courthouse," I said with confidence to the cab driver. Madly, he drove in and out of the traffic making me almost carsick. He slammed on his brakes right outside the courthouse. I got out of the cab wiser about the fares and handed him the exact amount of money.

Even though it was the middle of the night, there were still crowds of people gathered on the steps in front of the courthouse, mingling in conversation while puffing on cigarettes. Clouds of smoke seemed to obscure the path to the front doors. Holding my breath, I climbed the stairs and used all that was left of my strength, to open up the enormously heavy door, only wide enough so that I could squeeze through. And when I did, I stood in wonderment at another world.

The lobby was massive and beautiful with white and gray marble walls, huge granite pillars, art deco fixtures and brightly colored murals painting a story on the ceilings of the rotunda. It looked more like a hotel than a courthouse. In the center of the lobby hung an old brass round clock, marking the passing of time. I stared at it, knowing that we could not go back in time and start all over.

Beyond the clock, were two grand marble staircases connecting at the top and blending into one, leading to the second floor. For a brief moment, I had the impish thought to slide down the railings but I knew that if I did, I would have my own courtroom to find. The staircase definitely looked out of place, like it should be in a mansion, not a courthouse.

Feeling sheepish, I glanced around the lobby. Police milled around the security line with cups of coffee in their hand screening all those who entered the building as if they were guilty of a crime. Men, women, old and young, and from every ethnic origin, walked back and forth in the main lobby. Even though it was midnight, some mothers were pushing strollers while others were holding their sleeping toddlers in their arms. Benches were filled with people, some sleeping and others with their legs sprawled all over one another. And then there were clusters of people, standing talking quietly to one another and pointing to white pieces of legal paper that hung on the wall.

People coming in the courthouse, pushed me forward in the security line. The ones ahead of me placed their purses and backpacks on the conveyer belt as if they were old pros at this. Finally, it was my turn. I threw my black leather purse on the belt and watched two security officers scrutinize its belongings. Inside my purse was a tampon, a pad of paper, pens, crayon, a pacifier, my wallet and some small McDonald's toys that the kids threw in. The officer gave me back my purse and sternly said, "Take your cell phone and keys out and place them in the gray container." I did exactly what he said and gave him back the purse. He placed it on the conveyer belt and continued to look at its contents. He glanced at my purse and then looked up at me and smiled. I guess my contents were a bit different. I picked up my purse and walked into the main lobby. I stood for a moment taking everything in.

I felt overwhelmed as I watched the flurry of activity. To the left of the entrance, I noticed a round information desk. Two older women sat behind the counter and talked to one another while ignoring the people waiting to ask a question. I walked up to the desk and waited to speak with one of the women. "What do you want?" the gray-haired woman asked.

"I don't know what I am doing. Can you tell me where to go? My husband has an arraignment at midnight."

She mumbled something and then pointed down to a hallway. I looked at where she was pointing and by the time I glanced at her, she was talking to the next person. I guess my time was up, and I still had no clue as to what I was doing.

I glanced past the counter and saw a tall man exiting a room across from the desk. For some unknown reason, I ran over to him and said, "Can I ask you a question?" Without letting him respond, I continued. "My husband is mentally ill, and he took our son. We are from Michigan, and they drove here to New York. He has an arraignment at 12:00 a.m., and I have no clue where to go? Can you please help me?"

"Sure," he said. "Do you see the long white paper on the walls?"

"Yes."

"Those papers have the names, docket number, courtrooms and arraignment times listed. Go over and look for your husband's name and then you will see what courtroom he will be in. You are a bit early because I think they are running behind but you can sit on the benches and wait until his name and docket number are called."

"Thank you so much!" I gave him a hug, which he was not prepared for and I walked away. I glanced back to see him, and he was gone. I looked all around. It was as if he disappeared.

I walked over to the nearest wall. There were three other women standing huddled together. With their fingers scrolling down the long list of names, they spotted a name, whispered to one another and then walked away. Another woman came up and with tears streaming down her face; she took a tissue from her purse and wiped her eyes, straining to see the names. She glanced at me and said, "Do you want a tissue?"

"No, thank you. I am fine."

Pushing a tissue in my hand, she said, "You will most likely need one later."

I glanced at the paper and scrolled down the sheet as well. His name wasn't listed on the first page or the second or third. It was typed on the ninth piece of paper with other names beginning with the letter "S." Michael Sullivan. Docket Number DO14322. The arraignment time was midnight in courtroom 104. It seemed surreal seeing my husband's name on the list with the names of hardened criminals. I shook my head in disbelief, thinking about how one moment can change your life forever.

I sat on the bench outside of courtroom 104, waiting for the doors to open.

"Why are you here?" an older woman, sitting next to me mumbled.

"Me?" I asked, not knowing what to say.

"Yes, you. Why are you here?"

I wasn't in the mood to chitchat or tell a stranger my story, but she seemed concerned. Just giving her the short version, I said, "Well, my husband is mentally ill, and he abducted our young son and came to New York. My son was taken to St. Vincent's hospital and my husband was arrested. How about you?"

"Is your son okay?"

"Yes, he is safe and, thank God, nothing happened to him while he was on the streets. My sister is with him now."

"That is so good to hear. I am glad he is alright. My son stole a lot of money from people at the train station. He did it so that he could buy groceries for our family but then he got caught. It wasn't his first offense, so I don't know what will happen now."

"Gosh, I am so sorry."

"Do you want a cup of coffee?" she asked.

"No. Thank you. I am just going to sit here but thank you for asking."

I watched her walk away and thought about what it must be like for her to know her son got arrested because he was trying to feed her and the rest of her children? My mind then went back to Michael. I kept thinking about the future. What if he never gets well again? What if he can't work and can't watch the kids while I work? What if he tries to hurt me or worse yet, kill me? What if the kids and I have to go in hiding for the rest of our lives? Why didn't he take his medicine? That is all he had to do was take his medicine. The more I thought, the angrier I got. I should leave him here and let him navigate the system by himself. I need to be with Leo, especially after everything he had been through in the last 48 hours.

I called my sister. "Anne. I can't do this. After all he has done to us. He can rot in hell for all that I care. I need to be with Leo, not sitting here waiting for his arraignment."

"Mary, you love him. He loves you dearly, and he loves the kids so much. Remember the good times. We only need to take one step at a time. Later, there will be time to make decisions that are best for you and the kids. Leo is safe here, and we are just sitting together watching cartoons."

"Thank you, Anne for being here. I can't tell you how much I appreciate it."

As quickly as my anger rose, it dissolved instantly into guilt. I married him in sickness and in health, I thought to myself. I knew he was diagnosed with bipolar. What if he had a traumatic brain injury or if he was diagnosed with cancer? I would stay with him, undoubtedly. I thought about my parents who honored their vows through sickness and in health. They stood by each other's side when my father had many heart attacks and my mother suffered a stroke. They had each other's back even though life was not fair nor what they wanted or expected. I had a flashback of the recovery room after my dad had quadruple bypass surgery. He was groggy and just waking up. He held out his hand to my mom, and without any words being spoken, they just stared into one another's eyes and held hands. Their love was so powerful it made me cry.

The clock in the lobby struck midnight bringing me back to the painful reality. A woman in a navy blue jacket and skirt came out of the courtroom and opened the doors for all those waiting to come in.

It was a courtroom similar to the ones I saw on TV. There were aisles of benches that looked like the pews in church on both the right and left side. The benches in the back of the courtroom were crowded with men and women who were sleeping, staring at their watches or reading a book. There were fewer people sitting in the first few rows.

In the front, to the left were long wooden tables with people who looked like attorneys sitting behind them. In hushed voices, they wrote notes on the legal-size paper or they watched carefully as family members walked through the doors. Every once in a while, they would jump up, meet the family in the main aisle and lead them outside the courtroom to discuss the details of the case.

Also, in the front, two court officers stood guard — one in front of the judge's chambers and the other standing in front of the door to the holding cell. Both stood with their hands crossed in front of them. They were without expression and reminded me of the guards standing watch in front of a palace. The child in me wanted to walk up to them and try to make them laugh by making funny faces but I knew better.

Without understanding courtroom etiquette, I walked confidently down the center aisle toward the guards, swinging the gate that separated the courtroom from the judge. The moment my foot reached the other side of the gate, two officers came running toward me with guns in their hands shouting, "*Get back behind the gate, lady! Get back behind the gate.*" I was alarmed by their reaction and immediately looked over my shoulder for the out-of-control woman whom they were yelling at. There was no one behind me. Oh my God, they were talking to me.

I quickly retreated. With my hands in the air, my heart beating so fast I thought it was going to jump out of my body, I backed away. Embarrassed, I whispered an apology to the guard and said, "I just wanted to talk to the legal aid attorney who will be representing my husband."

"Over there," the officer pointed to the first row of benches. I scooted down the narrow aisle and asked to talk to the attorney representing Michael. A tall, thin woman with black hair tied in a bun smiled. I am sure she thought I was as crazy as my husband. She quickly came over to where I was standing and said in a quiet voice to meet her outside the courtroom.

Once we were outside the courtroom, she said, "My name is Karen, and I have been assigned to represent your husband."

"Hi. I am Mary. I am sorry about what happened in there. This is my first time in a courtroom. I must have looked as crazy as my husband."

"I totally understand." She chuckled and then became serious again. "As you know, your husband is very sick. From the records, it looks like he took your six-year-old son and drove out here to New York City, and they were walking the streets all night. Do you know why they were heading to New York?"

"I think he was heading to Germany but they didn't have passports. He is very delusional right now."

"Okay. Well, it looks like the police found them under the Brooklyn Bridge. It seems like your son was sleeping on the sidewalk while your husband was walking down the street. Is that right?"

"Yes. That is all correct. That is what the police told me. It has been a nightmare, but I am so grateful that we found them. Michael is a good father, he really is. He just got so sick." I wanted to convince her that he was so much more than his illness and that whom she saw was just a skeleton of who he really was.

She looked me in the eye and said, "If that happened to me, I would hate my husband and ask for a divorce right away." I paused and thought about her words. The whole experienced happened so fast. Within three months he went from being the man that I loved to be a man whom I feared.

"I love Michael, and I don't know where we go from here but right now I am the only one he has, and he is very sick. If he had cancer I would be by his side, and until he is back on his medications, I will still be there to support him in getting the treatment he desperately needs. He doesn't belong in jail; he belongs in a psychiatric hospital. Are they giving him his medications right now?"

"Not right now," she said. "He is in a holding cell, and they don't provide medications there. I understand what you are saying but I need you to understand that child endangerment is a felony in the state of New York. It is a very serious charge and this most likely will not be over quickly. Let me talk to your husband, and then we can decide what we need to do next."

I followed her back into the courtroom where the proceedings had already begun. It was quiet except for the sound of the judge and the prosecuting attorney. In the front row, there was a small room with windows. It was where the attorneys met with their clients before going before the judge. I saw Michael's attorney go into the room. At that moment, the door next to the judge opened. Out came a six-foot-tall man. He had his head down, and it was difficult to see his face. He was wearing a tattered, dirty white undershirt and khaki pants that looked for too big for his thin frail body. Handcuffs were on his hands and chains on his feet. An officer held on to his arm and guided him over to the small room. Like a bolt of lightning, I realized that the tall, thin man was my husband. He looked so different. I didn't even recognize him.

I couldn't see what was happening in the small room but after a few minutes, Michael shuffled out of the room. "The People versus Michael Sullivan," the bailiff announced. The guard proceeded to direct Michael in front of the judge.

"Do you solemnly swear to tell the truth, the whole truth and nothing but the truth so help you God?"

In a barely audible voice, I heard Michael say, "I do."

"How do you plea?" The attorney went up to the judge and whispered. I cocked my head so I could hear but it was just mumbling. The judge then said that the arraignment was postponed until tomorrow morning. I was so disappointed as I was ready to return home. I followed the attorney out of the courtroom. "I am so sorry, Ms. Sullivan. I wanted to help you and your family but your husband fired me. He said that he saw that we were talking, and he didn't want to have anyone who knew you. The arraignment is being postponed until tomorrow morning at nine."

"Thank you. He fired the last attorney as well. I am not sure what to do next."

"Another legal aid attorney will be assigned to him. He or she will talk with him prior to the arraignment. Hopefully, he won't fire that one."

Exhausted, I walked out of the courthouse. It was dark and still raining, a bit chilly for an early June morning. I hailed a cab and headed back to the apartment. I opened the door of the apartment to find Leo still awake, waiting for me. I crawled into bed with him and held him tight.

"Mommy, can you put the covers over our heads?"

"Sure."

"I don't want anyone to see us."

"Sweetheart, you are safe. I promise you are safe. I will hold you tight. Do you want me to sing our song?"

"Yes," he said in a quiet sleepy voice. "Taste and see, taste and see…," I sang as his eyes closed. It was difficult for me to fall asleep. I was just beginning to process what had happened, but I then began to focus on his breath and soon my body relaxed and I fell into a deep sleep.

The next morning, I got ready to go back to the courtroom.

Once again, I hated to leave Leo but I knew that he was in good hands with my sister. I brought him a bowl of Cheerios cereal, his favorite, and told him that I would be back before he knew it. He held onto the sleeve of my shirt and begged me not to go. I sat on his bed and spent a few minutes just holding and rocking him and telling him that I loved him so much and I would be back shortly. I promised him that when I got back, we could head to the airport and fly back home to be with Lucy and Elisabeth.

"Would you like that?"

"Yes. I can't wait to fly in a plane."

The cab dropped me off in front of the courthouse. I walked under the now familiar scaffolding, praying that it wouldn't give me more bad luck. I had experienced enough as it was. My mom used to say, "Don't walk under ladders or scaffolding or else something bad will happen." Something bad did happen, and I couldn't imagine it getting any worse but I wasn't going to challenge my luck. My weary body climbed the stairs outside of the courthouse. The doors seemed heavier than the night before as I pulled on the brass handle with all my weight. This time I felt like an old pro in the security line as I dug into my purse, pulling out my cell phone and keys and tossing them into the empty gray plastic container. I threw my purse on the conveyer belt and walk through the gate. I grabbed my stuff and headed back to the courtroom.

I opened the large doors and headed to the bench — this time staying behind the railing. I am sure the officers were looking at me, waiting for my next move but I was good and sat quietly waiting for Michael to walk through the back door. As I waited, I prayed for Michael to be safe, to be back on medication and to be the man I married. I kept staring at the emblem above the judge's desk. It said, "In God we trust." I focused my eyes on those words, took out my rosary, the one that my dad bought me when we were at the Vatican in Rome. "Hail Mary, full of grace. ..."

The bailiff called the court to order and acknowledged the

honorable judge who was presiding. All was quiet except for the attorneys, who were flipping through paperwork, talking to one another and getting up to talk to their client's family member outside of the courtroom. Then the door to the holding cell opened and a guard escorted Michael in. He was handcuffed to a waist-chain, and his feet were shackled as well. He shuffled over to the bench and sat down. He glanced over my way but he looked like he didn't recognize me. I looked back at him wanting him to see that I was the woman he married, whom he had children with and all of this was a terrible nightmare that we could work through if only he stayed on his medication. He remained void of emotion.

A new attorney was assigned to him and she met with him in a small room with windows on the far right of the judge. I tried to see what was going on in there and from the looks of it, it seemed to be going better than the night before. The attorney left the room, and the guard escorted Michael back to the bench.

"The People versus Michael Sullivan," the bailiff announced. Michael got up and slowly made his way in front of the judge. His attorney was at his side.

"Do you solemnly swear to tell the truth, the whole truth and nothing but the truth, so help you God?"

"I do," I heard Michael say.

"How do you plea?" the judge asked. The attorney jumped in and said, "Not guilty due to insanity."

"The case will be heard in two weeks. He will be transferred to the prison until the sentencing. There is no bail."

The sound of the gavel pounding not only echoed in the courtroom but in my body. The bailiff took Michael's arm and led him out of the courtroom. I was anxious to return to the old convent, pack our bags and take Leo home. I just wanted to be home. I ran out of the courtroom letting the heavy wooden doors bang shut behind me. I ran past the security guards and out the main entrance. With my hand in the air, I hailed a cab and headed back to Anne and Leo. When I arrived, I said, "Let's go home!" We threw our clothes into the suitcase and headed out to the busy street below.

"Mom. Hug me tight, please."

"Sure baby. I will hug you as tight as you want." The cab dropped us off at the front of the airport. Leo and I were heading on one airline and Anne another. I looked at her as we gave each other our final hugs. I didn't want to leave her; after all she was the one who got me to this point. I glanced back as she walked away and cried. "Don't worry, mommy. We will see her again." We stood in the ticket line, grabbed our tickets and once again went through security. I held on tightly to Leo's little hand almost in disbelief that we were finally heading home.

Walking briskly to the gate, I wondered how he walked all through New York. He was so little. It was astonishing that he could keep up with Michael. I looked at him; his small six-year-old body was filled with jittery excitement as it was going to be his first ride on an airplane. The anticipation seemed to distract us from the reality of what just happened. I was okay with that. We stopped by a gift shop and right away Leo was drawn to a miniature plane that was hanging in the window. He stopped and stared at it. So, I went in the shop and bought one for him and two for the other two at home. He played with it as we waited for our departure. Making swooshing sounds, he lifted the plane up high in the air and plummeted down to the ground. I was praying that our plane ride would not be as tumultuous as what his pretend flight was.

"Boarding now to Detroit, Michigan," the attendant called over the loudspeaker. We stood in line with the other travelers, tickets in hand. They checked our passes and directed us to the ramp that led to the plane. Leo skipped down the blue-carpeted path eager to see the inside of the plane. Once onboard, we found our seats and placed our luggage in the overhead compartment. Leo sat by the window, and I sat right next to him. I helped him buckle his seatbelt as he looked out the small window. He squeezed my hand tightly as we lifted off. We giggled as our stomachs tossed and turned with the increased elevation. He stared out the window and pointed to the tiny houses below and then to the white puffy clouds. "The clouds look like pillows," he said. He was captivated by the entire experience and listening to his oohs and ahs made the moment somewhat enjoyable. I had my baby back, I thought as I watched him.

Feeling relieved to leave the city that never sleeps, our plane landed on the runway in Detroit. I took a deep breath knowing that the next step of the journey would be even more challenging as the reality of what happened sank in.

WE LANDED AND HEADED UP the long escalator to the baggage claim area. The mid-day sun was shining through the window at the top of the escalator making it difficult to see. Vaguely I saw a man at the top waiting off to the side. The closer we got, I realized that the man was Andy, a dear friend of mine. He was waiting to drive us back home. I breathed in a sigh of relief knowing that I could let go and let him lead us to the car. I had become so vigilant and so used to being in charge that it was the first time in a few days that I could truly let go and breathe.

Leo was giddy on the ride home. He was cracking jokes and laughing hysterically.

"Want to hear a joke?" he asked.

"Sure," I said.

"What dog keeps the best time?"

"I have no clue."

"A watch dog."

We all laughed the deep belly laugh and then he told another one and another one. I don't know where he came up with these jokes but they sure did break the tension and allowed us to laugh.

As soon as we pulled into the driveway and came to a stop, Leo jumped out of the car. Lucy and Elisabeth, who bolted out of the back door at the same time, ran toward Leo. With their tiny arms around one another, they laughed so hard they toppled to the ground, one on top of another. It was so good to see all three of them together. I ushered them back in the house as if I was herding cattle. I saw my mom sitting there in the kitchen, and I ran over to her and fell into her arms. I felt like I was seven again when my parents came back from England after looking for a house, leaving us with our grandparents. I remember hugging her so tight, taking in the beautiful smell of her perfume. I did it again. I breathed in deep. She smelled so wonderful.

Andy brought in our bags, and I gathered the kids and asked them to come into the living room. We sat on the floor "crisscross applesauce" as they say in kindergarten.

"Where is daddy?" Lucy asked.

"Well, daddy is very sick, and he is staying in a hospital until he gets better."

I wanted to say, "Daddy is in jail because he did something really bad, and he won't come home for a very long time." But I knew that Michael was their daddy, their hero despite what he had done. They were way too young to understand the complexities of mental illness or what had happened or at least I thought so. As we sat in a circle, I paused for moment trying to conjure up something therapeutic to say but nothing came to my mind.

"What do you think happened to daddy?"

Right away Leo said, "Daddy's conscious is sick. He doesn't know how to make good choices."

After all my years of experience, I had never heard such a brilliant definition of mental illness.

Then Lucy said, "Daddy was in one room in his mind, and he loved us dearly and then he went to another room and the door was locked. He couldn't come back."

Flabbergasted with my mouth wide open, I said, "Yes. You both are right."

Elisabeth broke the silence by asking, "Did you bring anything for us?" We all laughed.

"We sure did," I said. Leo ran out to where the suitcase was. "Would you mind handing them out?" I asked.

"Sure," he said. His little hand slowly opened the zipper, and he pulled out the two small airplanes "This is the plane we flew on," Leo said as if it was the only thing that had happened to him.

After dinner, I tucked the kids in my bed, waited until they fell asleep and poured myself a glass of wine. I sat in the leather couch in the living room right next to my mom. "How are you, lovey?" she asked. I started to cry and what started out as a few tears trickling down my face turned into a hurricane of tears. I couldn't stop, and I just fell into my mom's lap. "It's going to be okay, honey; one step at a time. That is all we need to take. Just one step."

Then there was a knock on the front door. I peeked through the small window and saw my spiritual director from church, Sue. She asked to come in, and I invited her to sit on the couch in our living room. We talked endlessly about all that happened, and then she said, "Mary, we want to help you. Our prayer group talked about it, and we want to take care of things so that you can focus on the kids and whatever else you need to do with Michael. We are going to start bringing you meals three times a week so you don't have to worry about shopping for groceries or cooking anything. We will put a cooler on your front porch and then people will place the meals in the cooler so you don't have to answer the door. I have also arranged for teenagers, who go to private schools and need service hours, to babysit for you when you need to work and someone volunteered to mow the lawn for you and keep up with things around the house. Finally, a few of us are meeting at 7 p.m. tonight and I wanted to see if you could come along."

"Mom, do you mind if I go to the prayer group for an hour?"

Mom said, "Sure. I have everything covered here."

We drove to Sue's house and walked in the front door. Her husband escorted us into the peaceful garden room with white wicker couches and chairs. There were candles lit on the coffee table shining the light on the faces of the women in our prayer group. As soon as we gathered, Sue said, "Mary, we chose a theme for tonight but I want to pass it by you so that you are okay with it."

"What is it?"

"Taste and See."

Immediately I started crying because they had no clue that the song was so important to Leo and me. I started to tell them of the significance of that song, and they wept with me. The ringing of my phone interrupted the conversation. It was Leo. He said that he woke up, and he wanted to know if I would sing him the song. I asked him if it would be alright if my friends sang along with us, and in a sleepy voice, he agreed. I started to sing and then I heard the voices of my friends and then the precious voice of my son. During a time where I could have felt alone, I felt so surrounded by God.

The next few days were a flurry of activities. I had to establish some routine with the kids while picking up the pieces from what Michael had done. I had to call the bank and see how much money he withdrew and put a hold on our accounts except for my personal one. I also needed to call his job and request short-term disability. Next on the list was Michael's psychiatrist. I wanted to update him on all that happened and see if he could persuade the jail to start giving Michael medicine. I started to make another list in my mind similar to the one I made when we were hiking in the state park, but this one was different. I had only two weeks to get my life in order so that I could return to New York for his sentencing. I was "all in my mind," void of any emotion. I tried to keep our life as normal as possible, knowing deep down that there was nothing normal about our lives.

The next thing I needed to do was contact the director of a reading program for Leo. I had signed him up before everything happened, and I wanted to make sure he was still enrolled. When

I checked the avalanche of messages from my voicemail, there were 10 messages from the director of the program. She said that she hadn't heard from me, and there was another child who was on the waiting list. She wanted to know if Leo was coming. I called back right away and left a message telling her what happened and begging her to not give Leo's spot away. She quickly called back and said that she understood. She agreed with me that it was important for him to be in a routine to begin the healing process, and she assured me that there was a spot for him.

The following Monday I took Leo to the program while my mom stayed with the other two. I didn't realize how emotionally difficult this would be for Leo or me. We met the director at the classroom. She was waiting for us and wanted to personally introduce us to the teacher. I had sensed that she knew that I was nervous about leaving Leo after everything we went through. As the director showed Leo his seat, I explained to the teacher that no one could pick Leo up except me. I think I repeated myself about 10 times before I think she "got it." But, I didn't know what Michael was capable of behind bars and if he could even contract with someone to take Leo. I watched way too many dramas and had too many possible scenarios playing out in my mind.

It was time for me to leave but I didn't want to go. I went to Leo's seat, gave him a big hug, told him that I loved him dearly and told him that he was not allowed to go home with anyone but me. He shook his head. And then I gave him another hug and kissed him on the forehead. The teacher was beginning to speak, so I slowly walked to the door taking one last look at Leo. I felt so nervous as I lingered outside the classroom. Instead of going back home, I decided that I would sit outside the door and wait until the class was over.

When the class was over and the door was open, I jumped up from the hard tile floor, went into the room and was relieved to see his face. I gave him a big hug and helped him put his book away and, hand-in-hand, we left the school. By the following

Thursday, life was pretty predictable. My mom helped me keep the house clean, do laundry and grocery shopping. During the day, I focused on the kids taking them to the park, the zoo and the museums. After dinner, I snuck away to my private practice to see a few clients before the kid's bedtime.

I kept our routine of reading books, singing songs and then I lay with them until they fell asleep. Quietly I snuck out of the room and immediately got online trying to find ways to get Michael the psychiatric help he so desperately needed. Being in the legal system left me minimal control. Michael was placed in a large penitentiary in New York. I kept calling the prison trying to speak to the sergeant responsible for the ward Michael was on. Call after call, I asked to speak to him and finally out of the blue they transferred me to him. I think they were tired of me calling. The sergeant was shocked that I actually got in touch with him, as he didn't usually talk with family members. I wanted to see how Michael was doing and to see if he was finally on medication. The sergeant said that he was on medication but he had been in a fight with the other inmates.

"A fight?"

"Yea, the other inmates don't take well to those who have hurt children or put them in danger."

I couldn't believe that Michael was involved in a brawl with other inmates. He wasn't the type to fight or defend himself. I had a sick feeling in the pit of my stomach even imaging how he was doing in that prison amongst murderers, rapists and other hardened criminals. It seemed surreal that a few weeks ago he went from being an engineer in his plush office to an inmate behind bars.

Two weeks passed quickly, and I needed to get back to New York for his sentencing. I dreaded making the trip but I knew that I had to support him at least until I decided what to do and what was in the best interest of the kids. I made flight reservations and headed to New York. I felt much more confident as we landed and

I made my way to the "yellow" cab line. "Times Square, please." I had made a hotel reservation right down from the square. The cab driver dropped me off and said, "Stay safe." I got out of the cab and once again I was lost in a crowd of people trying to make my way to the hotel. People were tripping over my suitcase, and I kept apologizing. They all looked like they were having a wonderful time, drinking, dancing and standing in line for the theater. I was jealous that they had such a great life when mine was abruptly torn apart. I paused and I looked around at the crowd. I couldn't believe that only two weeks ago, Leo, with his small six-year-old feet, was walking these streets, trying to keep up with his manic father. It was truly a miracle that he didn't get lost amongst all those swarms of people.

I was restless that night not being used to sleeping alone. I either had my husband or my kids next to me, and I although I had always wanted the whole bed to myself, this is not quite what I meant. I turned on the TV and flipped channels and then I pulled out a book that was in my purse and began to read. My eyes read the words but I didn't even comprehend what they meant. I put the book on my nightstand and lay still — listening to my breath calmed me down. Within a few minutes, I fell asleep.

The next morning, I woke up early and got dressed. I grabbed a muffin at a nearby bakery and then took a cab to the courthouse. "The courthouse, please." Again, he drove quickly, and I was glad. "Here we are," the cab driver said as he dropped me off in front of the courthouse. I walked under the too familiar scaffolding, ran up the stairs and into the courthouse. Once again, I threw my keys and phone into the gray container and placed my purse on the conveyer belt.

This time, I had to climb the massive marble stairs to the second floor. The attorney had given me the number of the courtroom, so I knew where I was going. I walked down the long hallway wondering about all the people who walked the same path nervous as to how their lives would be changed by the pounding of the gavel. I walked to the front and sat in the first row. I looked around at all the people who were already waiting. There was an older gray-haired man who sat in the row across from me. He was slumped over with his unshaven chin resting on his chest. At first, I thought he was dead but then I heard him cough and was relieved. That is the last thing I wanted to experience — a dead body taken out of the courtroom. Life had been traumatic enough. I didn't need one more thing.

Behind me was a mom with her two adolescent children, a girl and a boy, sitting next to her. She was reading a Bible while the kid's poked and tickled one another. I wondered what happened to their loved one and what their story was.

Right before the bailiff was to announce the judge's entrance, an older man quickly slid into the row next to me, leant over and whispered, "Why are you here?"

"My husband is mentally ill, and he abducted our son. We found them. Why are you here?"

"My son ran over someone. He was drinking, and he was out of control. This wasn't the first time that he was involved with the law and I am sure it won't be the last. I will pray for you. Will you pray for me?"

"Of course," I said. "Thank you."

I was humbled that this man whom I didn't even know would pray for me.

"The State versus Michael Sullivan." Michael entered the room but this time instead of being in his tattered clothing, he was in a gray-and-white striped uniform. Cuffs still bound him, but he looked different, cleaner. Michael slowly turned around and looked my way but it looked like he didn't even recognize me. I knew that they said they were going to try to get him back on his medication but I started to question if he really was or if he was on the right medication or the correct dosage. He looked like he was heavily sedated.

His attorney spoke with the judge, and the judge sentenced

him to time in a state psychiatric hospital. I was glad that he was out of prison and relieved that he would get the medication and therapy that he needed to become stable or at least I hoped so. Once again, the gavel hit the table and I got up quickly with my suitcase in hand, heading to the stairwell. I ran down the stairs and out the front doors. I wanted to get to the airport to catch the next flight to Detroit. Within 30 minutes, the cab driver let me out at the airport. I ran in the lobby, checked in and went through security. I ran to the gate just as they were boarding. I wanted desperately to get home. Looking at my boarding ticket, I found my seat, sat down and buckled up. I never wanted to go back to New York again. I remember my mom saying, "One step at a time." The next step was for me to get home, take care of my kids and start rebuilding a life without Michael. Within hours I was home with my family, heating up the meal that was in the fridge and savoring the dinnertime chaos.

By this time, the kids were getting ready to go back to school. I had to meet with the principals of each school to notify them of what happened. By this point, I had a temporary restraining order even though Michael was in New York. It was only for a short time but I still needed to provide them with a copy of the document to keep the kids safe.

Michael called me every hour on the hour except for the nighttime. He had nothing better to do on the unit but stand in line at the pay phone and wait for his turn to call me. Much to my chagrin, his parents kept putting more money on the calling card. I didn't want him to call. I didn't want to talk with him or hear his voice; he still sounded so paranoid and I didn't have time to chat. While he was dialing my number, I was running around like a crazy woman trying to put the pieces of our puzzle together and find the missing ones.

In between the rushing around, there were days where the kids, my mom and I just drove in the country and soaked up the peace of the scenery, until the moment was interrupted by the ringing of the phone.

"What are you doing?" he demanded.

"The kids and I are taking a break and going to a farm out in the country."

"You are going to a farm while I am in here? You are supposed to get me out of this place!"

I pulled over to the side of the road and got out of the car so the kids did not hear me. I walked down the gravel side of the road, listening to him rant about how tough it was for him and that I needed to spend every waking hour helping him get out of the "hell hole."

I stopped and for a moment I saw the white puffs of dandelions all over. I leant down and pinched one at the stem, put it up to my mouth and I blew, mesmerized by how quickly the seedlings flew with one breath and how I was left with the empty stem.

"Mary, are you listening to me? You need to get me out of here NOW!"

By this time, I had it with his demands and his lack of empathy. I knew that he was still very ill, but I had always told him that his illness was my reality. I was done — just done.

"Michael, you are the one who got yourself into this mess. I am doing everything I can to get you out, but the kids and I need a break from the hell we just walked through. You have got to think about how this has affected us."

"Go on home, Mary, and get me out." I hung up on him as he continued to rant. As I walked back to the car, the phone rang again. I turned the phone off.

It was during the nighttime, I could finally breathe. I was free from the phone calls; free from the demands of three small children and free from the reminder of the hell we just walked through. I was still haunted by every sound in the house. I knew that Michael was around over 600 miles away, but my mind would not quiet. It stayed on guard, vigilant.

During the day it was different. There was an open child endangerment case on Michael in New York, and they contacted the agency in our city as well. I received a call from a caseworker that wanted to come to our home to interview us. He stated that a case had been opened, and he needed to interview my children, my mom and me. So in addition to surviving, I had to manage an open case where they were looking at my relationship with my kids, my parenting abilities and the cleanliness of our home.

I was fuming at this point since Michael was the reason that the case was open, and he wasn't even here to be interviewed. The whole meeting took over two hours. He asked every question possible and looked around our house. When he was ready to leave, he said, "Since your husband is in New York and will be for a while, there is no need to keep the case open. If you need to open a case when he is released, you can give us a call." I breathed a sigh of relief checking that one off my to-do list.

Eight weeks had passed and even though Michael was in a psychiatric hospital and supposedly on medication, he didn't seem to get better. He seemed more agitated and more paranoid than ever. He kept firing his psychiatrist stating that they were not helping him and instead they were plotting against him. I wasn't able to speak to anyone about it because Michael didn't sign a permission-to-release statement so I was in a fog as to what was happening.

I was only able to speak with his therapist at home though. I shared my concerns and he said that it might be better for him if we transferred him to a hospital nearby where he could be around his friends and family. The therapist thought that he would make a quicker recovery and return to the man he was.

I heard his words but I knew that even if he went back to the man he was, I was changed deeply by the experience. I was definitely not the woman I was before he left with Leo. After I hung up with his therapist, I felt sick. Here I was advocating for Michael to return home and to our lives, and I wasn't ready for that. I didn't want him back. I knew that he couldn't stay with us. He would have to find another place to stay until I was confident that he was better and then we would have to take it from there, step by step. I couldn't promise anything.

I thought about seeing him in the courtroom standing there, arms and legs cuffed and the glare of hatred he had in his eyes as he looked at me. It still made me shudder. Instead of honoring my feelings and what was best for me, I pushed them deep, deep down and began to focus on getting Michael transferred back. We were married, and I was committed to the vows. For some reason I put his needs before mine even though I knew that I was scared to have him back home.

I started to make phone calls when the kids were napping. I brainstormed with all the professionals and agencies that would help me in the transfer. I had quite the paper trail going on, documenting each person I spoke with, the date and time of our conversation, the details and the names and numbers of people they referred me to. I placed all the notes in a blue binder and kept it on my desk in my home office. Trying to get him transferred took my attention away from the indescribable pain and loss I was experiencing.

Finally, I was able to speak with the social worker at the hospital in New York. She understood that I was trying to get him transferred, but she didn't believe that it was the best course of action. She shared with me that he was very sick, and she was worried about what Michael would do if he were out of the hospital.

Michael on the other hand was telling me that he was better and didn't need to be in the confines of the hospital. He said that the people were making him sicker. I kept reflecting on the conversation I had with his psychologist from home. Maybe he would get better quicker if he was home and then we could file for a divorce.

I contacted the Office of Mental Health in Albany and then

the office in Michigan. I filed all the paperwork and contacted his therapist to tell him what I was doing. I then called the director at the psychiatric hospital near our home. Ironically, I knew him. He was in a few of my graduate school classes. He was a very compassionate man. I spoke with him and told him what happened. His question was poignant as he asked me if I felt safe if he was back here. "Oh yes," I said, not feeling confident in my response. He said that he would help get the transfer approved and then make the necessary arrangements to get him back home.

It took only about one week to process the transfer. The director told me the date and time of his arrival. He said that two officers would escort Michael to the airport and stay with him the entire flight to Detroit. He said that I could pick him up around two in the afternoon at the hospital psychiatric emergency room.

The day quickly approached, and I was a nervous wreck. I had already changed the locks in the house and a friend of mine hired a security company to install an alarm system. I checked all the windows and hammered nails in them so no one could open them from the outside. Now that he was coming back, I needed to do everything to keep us safe.

T HE DRIVE TO THE HOSPITAL for me seemed long, probably because I took every back route possible. I felt like I was driving to a meeting where they would tell me that I had a terminal illness and only a few days to live. My nerves were percolating to a boiling point, and I could barely breathe. I thought I was going into a full-blown panic attack. Why did I get him transferred again? The social worker advised against it. What am I doing? I pulled into the parking lot and drove aimlessly up the ramp to the first level, then the next level, and the next. I didn't want to park, I really didn't want to see him. I didn't want him to come home. I finally pulled into a space on the top level, open to the sky. I took a deep breath, sat a few minutes and then grudgingly got out of the car.

As I walked slowly into the entrance of the hospital, I dawdled every chance I could; at the stairwell, the elevator, the main sign that listed all the departments and the gift shop. I followed the sign pointing to the psychiatric emergency. Entering the automatic doors triggered me back to the moment I walked into hospital in New York to see Leo. I looked around the waiting room. Unlike the busyness of New York, there were a few people sitting in the cushioned chairs, glancing through magazines or checking their phones. I walked up to the receptionist who was sitting behind a closed glass window; she saw me and slid the window open. I leant in and whispered to her the reason for being there. In a way I felt embarrassed that I was in this situation. I was used to being the professional not the family member. She was kind in her response and directed me to the waiting room until my name was called.

A few minutes later, a nurse in blue scrubs opened the door and called my name. "Ms. Sullivan, the doctor is ready to see you." She held the door open for me and directed me into a small room. There was a beige sink in the corner and two chairs facing one another. I waited a few minutes before the director came in. It was good to see him again but not under this circumstance. We spoke about our journeys after graduate school and then he asked me again.

"Are you ready to see him?"

"I'm not sure."

"Take as long as you need, Mary. Let me check on a patient and I will then come back."

After a few minutes he came back to the room. "Let me ask you one more question: Do you feel safe?"

"I think so."

"Are you ready to see him?"

"Yes."

He motioned me to another room down the hall. Michael was sitting in a gray metal chair. He wore jeans and a light blue T-shirt. He was not as thin as he was in the courtroom but he still looked like a different person, not like my husband. He looked up at me and quietly said, "Hi." I said "Hi" back. I nervously signed his discharge papers, thanked the director, and we left the emergency room.

We slowly walked to the garage and rode the elevator to the top floor. "How was your flight?" I asked, trying to make small talk. What I really wanted to do was scream, "What in the hell were you thinking?" But I didn't. I stuffed that thought down right along the other ones.

"Well, they had me in handcuffs and people were looking at

me on the plane as if I was a terrorist. The officers were not nice at all, and they wouldn't even take my handcuffs off."

Once again, I wanted to scream, "What did you think they would do? You were in custody. You committed a felony, and the only reason it was reduced was because of insanity. You still committed a terrible crime. It was only three months ago that you abducted our son, were arrested and placed in a jail cell. You were an inmate at one of the toughest prisons and transferred to a psychiatric hospital. If it weren't for me, you would still be there." My anger was boiling again but I didn't say a word.

We drove home, and I could feel my veins popping out of my neck as I kept pushing down the thoughts and feelings, "Michael, I think it would be best if you go to your friend's house first. I want to prepare the kids for your return. I will drop you there and please thank them for me for allowing you to stay there until we figure things out."

I just wanted to get home to the kids. He got out of the car. I felt so relieved. I was shaking at the mere sight of him. I drove down our street and pulled over to the side. I knew I had to get my act together so I didn't upset the kids. With each breath, I could feel my pulse calm down, and I was ready to drive home. I pulled into our long driveway, got out of the car and the kids ran out of the back door and into my arms. I held them tight, breathing in their innocent smell.

"Let's go in the living room. I have something important to tell you." We sat on the carpet in a small circle. "Hey guys. I have something to say. Your daddy is back. He is on medication, and his brain is getting better but he won't be staying here for a while. He will be staying at his friend's house. What do you think?"

Lucy yelled, "I want to see daddy."

"How about you Elisabeth?"

"I want to see him too."

"Leo?" I asked.

"Yes, I want to see him."

"Okay. Then I will tell him to come over this evening. Remember, he won't be staying here."

"Will he ever stay here again?" Leo asked.

"I'm not sure of that. We will take it one day at a time."

A few hours later, Michael walked through the back door as if he were coming home from work. He didn't even knock, which seemed strange to me. I reminded myself that I needed to get in the habit of locking the doors. With him being gone so long, I felt that it was my house and when he walked in, I didn't feel safe anymore. I felt like he was invading my space. When the kids heard Michael's voice, they walked into the kitchen and stared at him. He knelt on his knees, with open arms

"Can I have a hug?" One by one they walked over to him and leant in for a hug. He hugged them for a while and then went with them into the living room. Getting down on the floor, he played with Legos with them while I sat on the couch, watching his every move and listening attentively to his words. I didn't want him to say anything that made the kids feel confused. My mom was standing guard in the kitchen.

After an hour, I told Michael that it was time for him to go back to his friend's house. He looked at me with a glare of anger, not wanting me to tell him what to do but thankfully he listened. Kneeling, he hugged each one of the kids and said goodbye. He looked at me, nodded and then left. I quickly went and locked the back door trying to regain some feeling of safety.

I gave the kids a bath and put them in their pajamas.

"Was it good to see daddy?"

"Yes," they shouted. "When is he coming back?" Lucy asked.

"I am not sure. Let's take it one day at a time, okay?"

I lay down on my bed. My insides were still shaking. Leo was on one side, Elisabeth was on another, and Lucy was holding on to my feet. We slept like that every night. It was only when I knew that they were fast asleep, I could wiggle out of the bed and go to the office to pay the bills or make some calls. If I stayed in bed,

I was vigilant to every sound in the house and I stared out the window waiting for the night to become day.

Michael came over to the house on a daily basis and I watched them from afar. He wanted to take the kids to a park but I wasn't comfortable in being in an open space where he could run away with one of them. He became resentful of my rules but I stuck to them, no matter how difficult he made it. I wasn't going to lose a child again. I wasn't going to go through that hell one more time. I said that the only way he could see them was if he came to our house.

He had every right to see the kids since the temporary restraining order had expired. There was no longer an open case through Jobs and Family Service since he spent so much time in New York, but the caseworker said that I could open one if he did anything that was dangerous to the kids or I. I kept the caseworker's business card in my wallet as well as one on the refrigerator door.

Weeks passed and I could sense something was different. He was becoming more belligerent and one night he refused to leave the house.

"Mary. You can't tell me what to do. These are my kids and this is my house. I have a right to be here and you can't tell me otherwise."

"Michael, you need to leave the house," I said in a firm voice. He refused. I walked into my bedroom where the kids were asleep, and I dialed 911.

"He is in my house. I have asked him to leave but he refuses. Please get him out of my house."

"Okay Ms. Sullivan. Someone will be right over.

While Michael walked around the kitchen making himself a sandwich, the officer knocked on the door. I showed him into the kitchen, where Michael looked at him and said calmly, "What do you need, Officer?"

"Your wife stated that you have been gone for a while and that she wants you to leave the house."

"I have every right to be here."

"Well, sir. You have been gone for six months, and she has the right to ask you to go."

"I will go but this isn't the end of it." Michael left, slamming the back door.

The officer looked at me and said, "Is he always like that?"

"Yes. He presents well but if you were to talk to him for a while, you would realize how sick he is."

"Ms. Sullivan, I would recommend that if you are afraid that you go down to the courthouse and get a restraining order. There will be a hearing within the month, and your husband will need to be present, but that piece of paper will protect you legally. He could still come up to the house but he would be in violation of the court order, and we could arrest him."

I took it all in, realizing that I needed to make that my next step. The officer left, and I called a friend and asked her to stay with us. I was still so shaken by his behavior as it reminded me of how he was right before he took Leo. I also knew that I needed to run down to the courthouse to file the papers the next morning and I needed my friend to watch the kids.

The next day I went down to the fourth floor of the courthouse and requested the paperwork for the restraining order. The woman behind the desk was kind and directed me to a sitting area where I could complete the forms. When I finished, I went back to the desk and she told me to wait until the magistrate was ready to hear my case. I didn't realize that I would have to go before a magistrate but I knew it was necessary.

I pretended to finger through the magazines but I was really listening to other people's conversations. One woman sat with her mother. She looked nervous as she played with her keys. "I think he is going to kill me if he finds out about this," she said to her mother.

"Honey, you need to do this to protect yourself."

"Mom. Sarah had a restraining order and that didn't stop Jack from stalking her. I also heard about a woman who had a restraining order and her ex-husband came up to her door, rang the bell and shot her, in front of her kids. That piece of paper means very little."

Wow, I never thought that Michael could get angrier at the filing of this paperwork or maybe by filing it, I would put the kids and I in more danger than we already were. Am I doing the right thing? I thought to myself.

"Sullivan. The magistrate is ready for you." I got up from the chair and walked into the small courtroom. "Do you swear to tell the truth, the whole truth and nothing but the truth?" With my right hand in the air, I said, "I do." The magistrate then proceeded to ask me why I needed a restraining order. I told him about what had happened and how Michael's behaviors had been more threatening as of late. He listened to me and said, "I will give you a temporary restraining order, and I will schedule a hearing on December 30th. Both you and your husband need to attend.

"What do I do if he becomes threatening here in the courtroom?"

"There will be plenty of police officers around, and I will make sure you are safe." I thanked him for his time, while all the while my mind was thinking about the upcoming hearing and how many different ways that Michael could hurt me, like in the parking lot or when I was walking to the courthouse. There were no officers out there. What if he killed me?

Even though I was scared, I left the room knowing that I did the right thing but still afraid as to what Michael would do when he received the subpoena in the mail. I went straight home because I just wanted to be around my kids. I wanted to do normal activities with them like reading books or playing card games. I wanted to forget about everything and most of all I wanted to stop feeling afraid. Michael called later but I did not pick up the phone. Instead, I turned on the house alarm, locked the doors and put the kids in the car. We drove to a friend's house out of town. I didn't want to deal with him at that moment, and I didn't want to be home if he were to bang on the door or break a window. I didn't know what he was capable of, especially since he did the unthinkable before.

Within a few days, Michael received the subpoena and left an angry message on my voicemail. I listened to it but deleted it quickly. I knew that I had to muster up all the courage I had to see him in the courtroom.

On the day of the hearing, I went down to the courthouse. I parked near the front doors, as I knew that there were police officers lingering outside. I quickly shoved the coins in the meter and then entered the building. As in New York, I threw my purse on the conveyer belt and watched the officers look through the contents. I walked through the metal detector and retrieved my purse. Taking the elevator to the fourth floor, I was relieved to see my attorney sitting there. I sat down next to her and listened as she spoke about what would happen next.

Michael came in about 20 minutes later. He walked right passed me and sat in the section of the waiting room farthest from me. When the time came, the magistrate walked out of the small courtroom and said, "Sullivan versus Sullivan." I jumped up as to not get to the door as the same time as Michael, and my attorney followed my lead.

I stared straight at the magistrate and only looked away when my attorney was talking to me. I didn't want to see Michael. I even struggled just hearing his voice. My attorney spoke for me and explained the situation. Michael came alone and did not have any legal representation. The magistrate asked him if he was seeing a psychiatrist and Michael proudly said that he didn't believe that he needed psychiatric help. He said that he was doing well without taking medication, and the reason that he was here is that his wife is hysterical and wouldn't let him see the kids. The more he spoke, the more obvious it was that he was mentally ill. The magistrate asked a few questions to both of us, and then he said he would grant the restraining order for a period of two years. He looked straight in Michael's eyes and said that he was not allowed to be within 500 feet of the kids or I and, if he did, he would immediately be arrested.

Slamming the gavel down, he said that the hearing was over. My attorney and I waited for Michael to leave the room, and we watched as he got on the elevator.

I felt at ease knowing that I had the legal document that would prevent Michael from coming close to the kids or me. At the same time, I was so saddened that I had to go to that degree to protect the kids and I from the man who I called my husband and they called their daddy. It still seemed surreal.

Michael got sicker soon after the hearing and, in a manic rage, he withdrew all the money in our retirement accounts. How he did it, I have no idea but he did, leaving me with no safety net in which to raise the kids.

Two months later, on Valentine's Day, the kids and I came home from dinner with my mom. I listened to the voice messages and was shaken to hear Michael's voice. Snickering, he said that if he didn't have the kids, no one would. I immediately called the police and filed a report. When was this nightmare ever going to end? Would it end in "death do us part?"

After a few months, I received a call from a friend of mine. "Mary, thank God you are alive. Are you okay?"

"Yes, why?"

"Michael called and said that you were dead, and he was going to all of the hospitals to find the kids. Where are you?"

"Oh my God, we are here at home but I need to get the kids and go to a safe place. Thanks for giving me the heads up. I will call you later."

Once again, the kids and I got in the car and headed to a friend's house for what I called a "slumber party." I tried to minimize the terror by talking about all the fun things that were planned. My friend tried to distract them with coloring books and Matchbox cars while I left messages for my attorney. After a few days of staying with our friends, we returned home.

Days turned into months and I hadn't heard from Michael. Life was getting back to a good rhythm. On a cool summer evening, the kids and I met a friend in a neighboring town. The town was having an open house celebration where all the little shops were open. It was a creative artsy town, and there was plenty to look at. It was also advertised that there was a woman who could read your aura. I thought that would be fun so we went into the shop and waited until it was my turn to meet with the woman. My friend took the kids to a bakery to get some cookies so I stood in line and mingled with the other customers.

As soon as it was my turn, the woman looked concerned as she stared in my eyes.

"Sit down," she requested. I sat down and she reached out to hold my hand.

"You are going through a lot, aren't you? I can see it in your aura."

"Yes, I have been walking a difficult path lately."

"I see," she said. "Do you know two men by the name of Nick and Michael? Nick isn't bad but he isn't right for you. Did you meet him by a lake or a pool?"

"Yes," I replied. "I met him at the pool at my Mom's condo. We both were single parents and in the process of a nasty divorces. Our kids went to the same school."

"Like I said," she continued, "he is a nice man but he is not good for you. And there is another man, one whom I am more concerned about. Do you have a large bush by your bedroom window?"

"No. I don't."

"Are you sure?" she asked again.

"Yes. I am sure," feeling frustrated that she was questioning me.

"Well, I really sense that a man named Michael is hiding

in bushes and looking through your bedroom window. He also is going to go up to your son's school. Is your son in a private school?"

"Yes."

"He is going to take him out for lunch."

Not believing what I was hearing, I persisted in telling her that it couldn't be true. Shuddering at the mere thought of what she said, I quickly gathered up the kids from the bakery, said goodbye to my friend and drove home. As I pulled in the driveway, I realized that there was a large rose bush in front of my bedroom window. I was speechless. I got the kids in the house, started the bathwater and numbly went through our bedtime routine. I locked all the doors and set the alarm. The kids and I went into my bed and, after we sang our songs, I lay frozen in fear. How did she know this? How did she know that I had a bush in front of my window?

A few weeks later, the receptionist at Leo's school called and said, "Ms. Sullivan, your husband called and said that he was going to pick up Leo."

Panicked, I thanked her for calling, grabbed my purse and keys and ran to the car. Speeding all the way, I picked up Leo and then went to the other schools to pick up Lucy and Elisabeth. We headed to the highway and drove as fast as I could away from town. Again, I told the kids that we were going on an adventure, and it was a surprise. Truly it was a surprise for me as well because I had no idea of where we were going. I just wanted to go far, far away.

After about two hours of driving, we stopped at a store and purchased pull-up diapers, bathing suits, pajamas, pool toys, juice and lots of snacks. We got back in the car and headed north. I drove until the darkness set in and until I felt it was safe to pull over. I noticed that there was a hotel off the next exit. I pulled into the well-lit parking lot and parked in a space closest to the hotel. I helped the kids with the belts on their car seats and with the shopping bags in our hands; we walked into the hotel lobby. We looked a little odd, as we didn't have any suitcases. We just had the plastic bags filled with our stuff. As soon as we got our key, we went to the room to change into our bathing suits. We then headed down to the pool and splashed around until the pool closed for the night. Tired, we held hands and walked back to our room. I changed the kids into their pajamas and we all jumped into the bed and pulled the covers over our head. They fell asleep so quickly but I was afraid to close my eyes. I didn't know where we would go next or how I would even afford another night in the hotel. I lay still in bed, holding on to my kids as tightly as they held on to me.

The next day we woke up and ate Pop-Tarts in bed as we watched cartoons. I went into the bathroom and called my friend Amy and told her everything that happened.

"Mary, come to our house. You will be safe here and then we can figure out the next step to take."

"Are you sure that we would not be an inconvenience?"

"Of course not. We would love to have you, and we have a room downstairs all ready for you and the kids."

"I can't thank you enough, Amy. Let me get the kids ready, and we will start heading home, to your home."

"Be safe," I heard Amy say as I hung up the phone.

The kids and I got back into the car and headed to her home. I played their favorite CDs and we sang every song. Before I knew it, we arrived at Amy's house. She and her husband were waiting at the door for us and came to the car to help me unload. Amy took the kids into an area where she had set out different toys and books.

While she kept them occupied, I spoke to her husband. We decided to call the school to see if he really did go to the school expecting to pick Leo up. The receptionist who had called me the day before said that he did stop by and he left rage-filled when he found out that Leo was not there. That is all I needed to hear.

Amy's husband Bob suggested that we file a complaint stating that Michael violated the restraining order. I knew I needed to do it or else I would have to live in fear not knowing what would happen next.

Bob and I went down to the police station and filed a complaint. The officer who filled out the paperwork said that they would go to Michael's friend's house and arrest him. I didn't know how long he would stay in jail, but I knew that it was at least long enough so the kids and I could return home.

A few days later, he was released from jail. Michael left the city with no trace. We both had already started the divorce process, and I chose to continue it. I wanted it all to be over. I had an inkling that he was either living in his car or living on the streets. Once in a great while, he would call and leave a message stating that he wanted to talk to the kids. Other times, I would get a call from a police officer stating that they arrested him for unruly behavior. Weeks went by and the court date to finalize the divorce approached quickly. Amy, her husband, Bob and I went down to the courthouse and waited for the judge.

The judge called me into her courtroom, and I explained why Michael wasn't there. She asked me a few questions, had me sign a few papers and it was done. I was divorced. It was strange because within a few minutes, it was all over. It took so long to get married; the marriage preparation retreat, meetings with a couple at church, a talk with the priest — yet it was so quick to get divorced. I felt relieved but sad. My dream of being married turned into a nightmare that ended in divorce. It was time for me to rebuild my life.

Turning tragedy into holiness

S O THAT'S MY STORY. THERE is no ending; there is only living with being changed by what happened in a good way. We have a choice to be a victim of our story and allow it to define us or we can be open to all that has happened and allow it to transform us. Easier said than done but being stuck in our own story thwarts our ability to grow and become fully who we are called to be. It is solely our choice to allow the experience, as painful as it is, to transform us and the one way we can choose to do so is to learn the lessons and pass them on.

Lesson one: It is what it is

Even though denial seems like a wonderful thing, it is only a temporary state. Denial protects us until we no longer need to be protected. It hides the truth like a well carved out mask. Everything looks good on the outside and as long as we wear the mask, we too believe that everything is good and we will do anything to make sure it stays that way.

If there is a question of doubt, we rationalize it by saying,

"Every family has something," "There are people worse off than me" or "If I only tried harder, things would be different." We even try to convince others by saying, "We are doing great" or "We have never been happier." But in the stillness, we know that things aren't okay and we can only hide from the truth for so long before the mask begins to crack and the truth breaks through. The truth becomes unavoidable because it is bold, persistent and loud.

There is a good thing about denial, though. It gives you the time and the grace to gather all your courage and determination to face the inevitable. The reality is there, and it is not going to go away. You know it. And there comes a point in time when you no longer want to hide. You know it is time to face the ugly hard truth no matter how much it hurts and what unknowns it brings to your life. You are ready to own your own story as frightening as it is but to stand strong and without shame to your truth. Staying in denial disconnects us from others and ourselves. We suffer alone yet yearn for understanding, acceptance, support and assistance. Standing in our own truth, as difficult as it is, allows healing and it connects us with others, allowing them to companion us while at the same time, giving them permission to do the same.

Don't let anyone tell you when it is time to face the truth. It is your timing, only yours. When you are ready and only when you are ready, you will be able to take off the mask and have the eyes to see and the strength to deal.

It seems like I have lived my life in the house of denial. It was so much easier to think that everything was fine than to see the harsh reality and that was my husband was very, very sick. I knew deep down that he had a serious illness, but I didn't want to admit how serious because I didn't want what we had to stop, even though what we had was tough and exhausting. He was the first man who made me laugh hard. He was intelligent and faith-filled. He was everything I was looking for — except his illness. So, I held the flashlight on the times that were wonderful, and I turned it off when things looked frightening.

Even when he was experiencing an episode (and I couldn't turn the flashlight all the way off) I still stayed in another layer of denial. I convinced myself that love could conquer all and that my unending support in addition to my therapeutic background would be enough to keep him and his illness on track. In my mind, all I needed to do was to challenge his paranoia with truth and that would be enough for him to come back to reality. My undying hope was that if I tried hard enough, his illness would go away, and we would live happy ever after. That didn't happen. What I learned was that it wasn't about me. It was about his illness and the choices he made to stay well, like taking his medication and attending therapy.

Someone once told me, that you can't speak logically to someone who is insane. It is a like a foreign language; they just don't understand. But I tried over and over and over again to reason with him, to help him to understand. Time after time, I begged him to make different choices but to no avail. I pleaded for him to understand how his choices affected our family. I begged him, I cried, and I even threatened to leave. But he couldn't understand my language — not that he didn't want to — his mind simply could not process the thoughts.

What denial never showed me was that Michael's illness was bigger than our love and louder than the denial. Nothing I would do or say would change that. Bipolar has a mind of its own and, like a tornado, it leaves considerable destruction in its wake. And this awareness led me to the second lesson: you know when you know.

Lesson two: You know when you know

After I came to grips with the fact that Michael was a very sick man, and that my love for him would not affect his choice to take his medications nor would it change how his psychotic thoughts would affect me and the kids, I was challenged with the second lesson: you know when you know. It didn't happen overnight but there came a point when I knew without a doubt that things had to change.

Prior to the knowing, there were many years of what I called "analysis-paralysis." I looked at my marriage, family and his illness from every angle. I listened to the "shoulds" of our marriage vows and our family's expectations that we stay together till death do us part. I felt the overwhelming and suffocating burden of trying to support him through his episodes while trying to take care of our children and myself. I even spoke to my spiritual director about it and prayed the rosary every night. I spent countless hours writing in my journal, reading books about living with someone who suffered from a mental illness, attending NAMI meetings and talking to my therapist.

And then there were times where I became quite frightened at the mere thought of leaving him and all the "what ifs." What if we divorced and he committed suicide? How do I tell the kids? How do we move on? Even though I knew that I was not responsible for his choices, there would still be a part of me that would feel guilty and how would I live with that? This stage of the process was exhausting but I needed to make sure that I thought through everything so that I could make the best choice for the kids and me.

And then this deep sense of knowing often shows up unexpectedly. It is an undeniable, percolating sound of truth coming from within. No questions, no hesitations, you just know. Everything that you experienced prior, the forbidden emotions you have repressed and the all-night ping-pong battles of pros and cons have all led you to the moment where you know that you will take a different path.

It is often referred to as intuition, inner voice or God, and it shows up differently in each one of us. It can be an inner sense of relief, a visible sign, a "aha" moment, a persistent hunch or a tingling within the body and the trembling within our soul. The voices of knowing do not criticize, shame or blame, they simply communicate to your truth.

Realizing and accepting your truth is not an easy thing do it. In fact, it is painful, horribly painful. What used to be comfortable no longer comforts and what used to protect no longer needs protection. And with time, we finally reach the point where the pain of staying the same is greater than the fear of the unknown. You just know.

For me, the truth came when we were hiking on a wooded trail, and I saw the fork in the path. I knew at that very moment I would have to choose to continue the way that we were or take a new path. If we continued the same path, I was pretty sure that the stress would eventually lead to a heart attack and I would die, or the alternative was that I would go crazy myself. Crazy wasn't an option because the kids needed one of us to be sane. And it obviously had to be me. As I took each step toward the fork in the path, I was struck with clarity where there was none before. It was as if a lightning bolt hit me and I knew without a doubt what I was going to do. It was as if I heard a strong voice saying, "You are going to walk away from your husband and build a life with your kids. It won't be easy, but you can do it." As daunting as this revelation was, I knew it was the truth and in a way I was relieved to finally know that the months of tossing and turning at night was over. I needed to put my big girl panties on and start walking this uncharted course.

At the same time the pain of knowing is excruciating. Not only was I grieving the loss of my husband to the illness, but I also was grieving the loss of him in my life and the lives of our children. What I dreamed for our future was shattered in the knowing. There wasn't a lot of time for grieving though because I had so much to do to prepare for the next step. I knew that I was where I needed to be and when I was ready to grieve, I would have the time and space to do so.

Until then, I had to trust that I had all that I needed to prepare for the third lesson and that is taking one step at a time.

Lesson three: Take one step at a time

The first lesson taught me to be present to what is and not what you want or need it to be. The second lesson taught me how to listen to my body and my soul and to trust that inner voice that told me in a loud and rather confident way that I needed to make a change. Once I came to grips with the truth that change is inevitable, I felt totally overwhelmed. You may become completely blindsided by the feelings you have been repressing throughout the decision-making process. Self-care and self-preservation begins with staying focused on the present and only the present.

Making the decision to leave was one thing but actually coming up with a plan in a moment of utter chaos was another. After he took our son, I was paralyzed in shock unable to think clearly or even put a coherent sentence together. I couldn't believe what happened nor did I have a clue as to what to do next. After a period of time of numbly staring into space, I gathered myself together and began to think about what my next step would be. Just acknowledging that became the first step. Remember, you don't need to know all the steps right now, just the first one.

As long as I put my energy into the what ifs, it thwarted my ability to be honest with the "what is." Trust me, it is possible as long as we take one step at a time. Our point of power is where our feet are — in the moment. If we try to look ahead, it all becomes too overwhelming, and if we try to look back, it keeps us stuck in the past where we literally have no control. Standing in the present allows you to make conscious choices as to what needs to be done at that very moment. I promise you that when you need to know the next step, the next step will reveal itself to you. It will be there, ready for you to stand on and it will give you the wisdom to know what to do. One step after one step after one step, lead you to and through change. Once you have taken a few steps, the next lesson reveals itself: You must believe to receive.

Lesson four: By receiving you experience grace

This lesson was one of the most difficult lessons for me to learn. Soon after we returned from New York with Leo, I was keenly aware that I couldn't do it all alone. I was trying to take care of the kids, keep my work going, pay the mountain of bills that were accumulating not to mention the need to manage Michael's legal issues and make sure he was on the correct medication.

One evening after I bathed the kids and they were quietly playing in the other room, I went into my bedroom and closed the door. I fell to my knees and, with my hands in the air, I yelled, "Dear Lord… give me strength." I knew I couldn't do it myself and I needed to ask for help. Gratefully, my friends were one step ahead of me and arranged meals, babysitting and anything else I needed, but I still had to receive and that in itself was daunting. I was always the giver, the one who made meals for others, sat with them at the hospital or listen to their stories of grief. I was not the one who needed help, asked for it or was comfortable in receiving.

I am not sure if I felt unworthy of the attention and help, or if I didn't want to feel incompetent or be perceived as needy, weak or a burden. I was raised with the belief that what happens in your family stays in your family and that you need to pick yourself up and move on. I had to quickly cast those beliefs aside and graciously open my arms and mind to receive.

I struggled, really struggled. I felt guilty that while people were making meals for us, their family was waiting for a meal to be set on their table. I knew that they were all so busy and really didn't have time to take on one more family but they did. One by one, men and women came to our door with groceries, food and offered to help with the yard. I was shocked beyond words that people cared so much for the kids and I. One wise woman noticed my discomfort and said, "You aren't used to receiving, are you?"

I replied, "No."

And then she said, "I understand but by receiving, you experience grace."

I sat with that for a while and pondered the profoundness of what she said. "Grace" as defined by Merriam-Webster dictionary is the "virtue coming from God" and "virtue" is defined as courage and strength. It was as if each time someone helped my family, they gave us God's gift of courage and strength.

And believe me when you are going through a crisis, you need a little bit more of courage and strength and a bit more of God. It is as if everyone has a bucket within, and when we are in crisis, our bucket is dangerously depleted. In order to continue to navigate through the thunderous storms ahead, we need to receive. We need all the courage and strength we can get and by receiving, we are refilling our bucket. We are not self-centered for asking for help but instead centered in self when we know what we can do and what we can't do. We are not a burden, but we are carrying a burden that when shared with others, allows us to continue to walk.

Once I allowed others to lift our family up when we couldn't walk, I was faced with the next lesson and that was healing.

Lesson five: Healing happens in one's own time

Taking one step at a time often doesn't seem enough. We are anxious to take as many steps as possible and as quick as possible so that we will no longer feel the pain. We want to fast forward our lives to a different place, but that is not how life works. There is a natural process to everything and I believe that we are where we need to be until we have learned the lesson. The process also gives us time to gather all our strength and courage we need in order to take the next step. When we are ready and only when we are ready, the step will then appear. This applies to healing as well. I wanted the kids to heal immediately and I was willing to do anything I could to help facilitate it. So I did what I knew how to do and that was to enlist the help of therapists, many therapists. I over therapized the kids to be honest. I had them in cognitive therapy, play therapy and art therapy. It was all going well until we went to one session with the art therapist.

As I was processing the kid's scribblings, I was interrupted by the therapist. She beckoned me to meet her outside of the room. Immediately I had flashbacks as to when I was second grade and I was in trouble for talking too much. The teacher motioned me into the hallway and had a "come to Jesus talk" with me. Even being an adult, my palms were still sweating and my heart was beating as I walked into the narrow hallway. What could she possibly be ready to tell me, I pondered.

"Mary. You want the kids to heal now, right?"

"You bet I do. I am ready to move on and to re-build our own lives."

"I understand, I really do. But here is what I know to be true: You and the kids will heal when you are ready and only when you are ready to heal. Everyone will do it in their own time and their own way."

Feeling utterly deflated by the truth and with tears in my eyes, I walked back into the room and joined the kids at the table. She was right. I couldn't command them to heal nor could I command myself to heal. We had to do it in our own ways and in our own time.

She was right. Throughout the years, the kids processed what happened at different times and different ways. Leo wrote about what happened in an essay at school and he was quite open about it when talking to his friends. Lucy posed questions usually when he and I were driving somewhere together, and Elisabeth talked about it a lot and looked at pictures. It was uniquely their own grief. And each year they viewed the incident with new eyes and a more developed brain that could process it all differently.

I also wanted the kids to know about their father and how wonderful he was while teaching them about his mental illness and how it affected his behaviors.

I spent a lot of time, reminiscing with them and telling them how much daddy loved them and how proud he would be of them. I wanted them to know that without a doubt that their daddy loved them more than they would ever realize and that he didn't want what happened to happen. Michael was not his illness but when his illness showed up, his behaviors were frightening. Even though I was in a pinch financially and emotionally after everything that happened, I did not want to say bad things about him because he was the man I loved, and he was their father, a part of their genetic makeup.

As a parent, the last thing I wanted for my kids to experience was fear but I needed to tell them that daddy's behaviors were not okay and that they were not to go with him if he came to the house or came up to him at the park. Even though we had a restraining order, I wanted to give them the tools to protect themselves, and it made me sad that I even had to give them the tools.

Mental illness is confusing enough for me to understand, and I couldn't imagine in their little minds how they understood it. Kids are concrete thinkers and mental illness is not concrete. They were unaware of all the ups and downs of his illness when we were married as I tried to shelter them from it. We tried to keep our conversations about jobs, money and medication mainly in the bedroom where they could not hear, or we would talk after they went to bed. I am sure though that they picked up on the tension and that was one thing I could not control. Each one developed their own stress-related symptoms such as the constant clearing of the throat, scratching of the skin or the social anxiety when being with anyone other than our family. With time those symptoms disappeared, but it took a lot of steady routine, nurturing and new traditions to give them the feeling of safety and normalcy.

As they got older, I wanted them to know that everyone has a story that leads them to the place that they are today. When we would see a homeless person holding a sign asking for money, I would tell them that that person was someone's child, brother, sister, aunt, uncle, husband or wife. I spoke about Michael and how when he was really sick, there were times that he was homeless. So we collected new and used blankets, sleeping bags and pillows and gave them to the homeless on the streets, under the bridges or on park benches. We went down to a shelter for those who suffer from mental illness and served them a hot meal. I felt that these experiences aided our healing and gave us control over something that was so out of our control and that was mental illness.

And as to my healing, it was put on the back burner until much later in life. I used every ounce of energy to take care of the kids and manage our expenses. I didn't have time to lose it or fall apart. I had to push that aside until I knew that they were fine, and it was time to talk care of myself. Writing helped me a lot and helped to sort through the fear and chaos we endured. Other times I would go to bed and cry because life seemed too hard, and it wasn't the life I had planned. But with each year, I felt a bit more freedom and a little bit more hope. Even though my life wasn't what I thought it would be, I kept plugging along. Eventually, this led to the sixth lesson.

Lesson six: You can only control that which is in your control

Michael took away our feeling of safety, and he also took all our money, but what he didn't take was our spirits. I always heard that you can only control that which is in your control and the rest you have to let go of. What was in my control was making life as normal and fun for the kids even on a very limited income. What was out of my control was what other people thought of me and what Michael was doing.

I always told the kids we might not have a lot of money, but we were rich in spirit. During one Thanksgiving, we sat around our dining room table. Holding hands, we prayed together and then I encouraged the kids to add their own prayers. Elisabeth chimed in, "I pray for all of the poor people." I stopped, thought about what she said and replied, "Honey, we are the poor people." She looked at me in shock. She didn't know that, though, because I was fiercely determined to turn our challenges into adventures, even when it came to money. I wanted to respond to the stressors in a way that protected the kid's childhood.

I continued to work on developing my private life coaching practice. But I needed to spend most of my time at home to make sure we were safe. I didn't want to be too far from their schools in case something happened. I usually had enough money to pay my bills but at times "I stole from Peter to pay Paul," as that old saying goes. There were a few occasions when I didn't have enough money to pay my utilities. When the electricity was turned off, I would pack the kids in the car and head to the nearest grocery store that accepted late utility payments. With three small children in tow, I talked to the clerk while bribing the kids with M&M's. I paid the lowest amount I could, and she assured me that the electricity would be turned on in an hour. We drove around looking at different neighborhoods, singing songs, reciting the alphabet and playing too many games of "I Spy."

When the kids were ready to rip off their safety belts and get out of the car seats, I knew it was time to head home. Praying all the way that the electricity would be turned on, we drove into our driveway and low and behold, the lights were on. "Wow. What a fun adventure, hey kids? Now who wants to watch a movie and eat popcorn?" We went inside, snuggled on the couch under the quilts and watched a movie until it was time to go to bed. We made it one more month.

I remember hearing about the importance of not allowing the experience to seep into our every thought and behavior. It would have been so easy for me to stay a victim, wearing my scarlet letter on my chest but that wasn't me. After losing so much — my husband, my family as I knew it to be, all our savings and our emotional and physical security — I realized what was truly important: my children.

I also became incredibly clear about the differences between "needs" and "wants." Having groceries in the pantry was a need, having a warm home to come back to was a need and having gas in the car was a need. Anything else, I could let go of. But the most important need, for me, was going into my children's rooms, sitting on the edge of their beds and watching them breath. That was the greatest need of all, one that I never again took for granted.

One very cold and snowy December day, Elisabeth and I went into a store to buy some gloves and hats. We passed the man who stood outside ringing the bell for the Salvation Army holiday collection, without gloves. We walked in and then walked out realizing how cold he must have been. Elisabeth suggested that we buy him some warm gloves. With whatever change I had left over in my purse, we went back in and bought him gloves and a hat. At that moment, everything made sense to me. We were blessed to have a home, a roof over our heads, food for our bodies and food for our souls and eyes that see the need of others. No matter how difficult our situation was, we were still blessed. And with many blessings, we are called to give. This led to the next lesson and that was appreciate the small moments because within those moments are moments of holiness.

Lesson seven: Appreciate the small moments

The next lesson I learned was to not take anything for granted and to stop frequently to truly take the moment in, to absorb it and to be fully present. You never know when it will be the last. I know that sounds dreadful, but it is true. Life changes in a second.

When I was about seven, I asked my mom, "When do you know it will be the last time?"

"Last time for what?" she asked.

"I mean the last time we will play hide-and-seek or the last time I will play with my dolls. I want to know because I want to really appreciate it."

Mom thought about it and said, "We never know, Mary."

Fast forward many years and I still ponder about the "last times." I wish I knew when would be the last time we would sit around the table as a family and say what we liked about our days. Or the last time we'd celebrate Christmas together watching the kids open their gifts. Or the last time we would watch a movie together, cuddled up on the sofa. It all went so fast and now I am taunted with the thought that there was so much I didn't appreciate.

The truth is we never know when the last time is. I learned how to be truly present to the moment and not to waste time on things that really didn't matter. I learned to tell people how I really felt, and I chose not to hold grudges. Grudges take up wasted space in your heart and consume too much precious time, and time is so short. I also learned to give power to that which gives life and not what takes it. I said yes to all I wanted to do, and I said no to that which left me empty. By saying, "No more," it gave me more time to take care of my family and myself. I realized that was my most important priority. Nothing was greater than my children and making sure that they had the most normal life I could give them. I chose to make choices that affirmed that value. Because you never know when a moment can change and what you took for granted is no longer there to behold.

With time, I learned to pause the moment and really take it in for all that it is worth. I pressed the pause button when I opened the door to their bedrooms in the morning and saw their little faces delighted to see mine. I pressed the pause button as I listened intently to their laughter and relished in the pure joy that was woven in each rise and fall of their voices. I also pressed the pause button when they graduated from preschool, elementary, junior high and high school amazed how time had flown by. But no matter how old they were I pressed the pause button as I checked in on each one of them after they fell asleep, basking in their innocence and watching their breath go in and out in a rhythm reserved only for holiness. And in that moment — that very moment of silence — I thanked God for allowing me to be their mom because they have been the greatest gifts I have ever received.

Sometimes tragedy puts life into perspective, giving us a second chance to appreciate all that we have been given. It jolts us into never taking anything for granted and leaves us with eyes that see and know what is truly important.

When I mastered this lesson, I was ready for the next: forgiveness.

Forgiveness is not about them but about you

Forgiveness is such a challenging act and sometimes you will need to do it again and again and again. (Did I say again?) Just when you think you have forgiven, something or someone will take you back to the moments of anger and hurt, and you go through the entire process again. It's okay. We all do it but eventually you will get there. When you do, it is a wonderful feeling because you will be transformed by the process, and you will be able to truly move on.

Remember, forgiveness is not about the person who hurt you. It is about you, only you. By forgiving, you are choosing to not allow that person or the emotions to control your mind, occupy your precious time or stop you from moving on. Bitterness is like an octopus, wrapping its tentacles around you, suffocating the joy out of life. Instead of focusing on the moment, you are absorbed and consumed by the past emotions of intense anger and rage. Rather than being open to new experiences, you obsess about the past — what he/she said, what happened, your feelings. You repeat the story over and over again to no avail. The more you tell the story, the more you become your story; the more you stay in a quicksand of victimhood, the more your life becomes tied to the one who has hurt you. It isn't about who is right or who is wrong; it is about honoring your feelings and allowing them to lift you up away from the victim role and to a place that is more empowering. You own your story — your story does not own you. You can change the ending by allowing the process to change you.

There is definitely a time and place for feeling and, as weird as it feels, it is important to honor those feelings. What happened happened and there is no denying that someone else's words or behaviors have affected you. Allow yourself to name the feelings and let them roll right through you. Create a ritual that will help you feel, like journaling, drawing or writing a letter (and not sending it.) When you begin to feel better, you are done and can start thinking about all the ways this experience has changed you for the better and how you want to live your life from this point forward.

It was hard to forgive Michael for all that he did to my kids or me. Believe me, I tried to forgive but it wasn't easy. It took a long time until I realized that my anger at him no longer served me. With time and healing, clarity set in, and I realized I was angry at his illness. Even though he made the choice to not take medication, he did not make the choice to have psychotic or paranoid thoughts. And if I put myself in his shoes, I would probably listen to my thoughts as well.

I knew that Michael loved us, and I am often reminded of what Lucy said, "He was in one room in his mind and he loved us dearly and then he went to another room and the door was locked." My anger dissolved immediately into sympathy. I felt bad that he had such a devastating illness that affected his life and the lives of all who loved him. And I needed to use this experience to make me a better person. There was a life to be lived and I was determined to do it to the fullest for the kids and I.

Utter holiness

As I have been writing this book, my friends have asked, "What is the end of the story?" There really is no end, because life goes on. Michael was extradited back to the city and appeared before the courts. He continued to go on and off medications and at times his behaviors were quite frightening and dangerous to the kids and me.

I tried to make life as normal as I could despite all the stressors. I attended Cub and Girl Scout meetings, I helped with the school's holiday parties, watched countless soccer, baseball, basketball and volleyball games and, in between that, I worked as much as I could to pay the bills.

Ironically, my mom used to say when I was young, "There by the grace of God goes I," and I used to mock her behind her back. But there was truth in that statement. In a moment, my life changed. I went from being married, a mom of three to a mom of missing child, a divorced mother and a mother who had a suitcase in the back of car ready to leave in a split second.

Years later, as life calmed down, I was able to take the suitcases out of the trunk. We began to breathe, laugh and just enjoy the simplicity of life. My kids got older and as I watched them grow and go through their milestones, such as the first day of school, first communion and confirmation, I grieved because Michael wasn't there to celebrate with us. I grieved that my children did not have a father figure. Yet I was so proud that we made that it that far. We went from surviving to actual living.

The kids and I created a family bucket list and checked off different experiences every year. We swam with the manatees in Florida, stood in awe at the sun setting in the Grand Canyon. We had deep respect for the men and women who carved Mount Rushmore and continue to carve the Crazy Horse sculpture. We hiked the Black Hills of South Dakota, the red rock formations in Sedona, Arizona, and the beautiful mountains in Tennessee. Being able to travel as a family kept us close. While traveling we were forced to be with one another and, to be honest, we enjoyed every minute. When we got back from our trips and everyone had their own activities, I missed them.

I still struggle with the thought of letting my kids go, as every mom does. But for me, it taps into that deep hole of helplessness when I realized Leo was gone. I know I am in a different place now but at times, it still shakes me to the core. There are times where I wake up in the middle of the night, thinking that someone is in my house. With my cell phone in hand ready to dial 911, I search every room just to find out that the noise was coming from the rain hitting the windows.

I learned from that experience that life can change so quickly and what is important is what is right in front of us now. I wasn't going to give power to the past because I couldn't change it, but I could give power to how I would allow the experience to change me.

The final challenge for me was for forgiving myself for breaking my vows and for leaving my husband when he was sick. I already forgave Michael, which was easy to do, because I loved him and because he was so ill. Forgiving myself was another story. I often looked at what other families had to go through with diagnosis of dementia, ALS and pancreatic cancer. They continued to walk together. But I didn't. I chose a different path. I knew in my heart that it was the best path for the kids and I, but I still felt guilty.

And then one night I had a dream. A dreamt that I was sitting with God, telling him about why I had to break my vows. Breaking down in tears, I said to Him, "I tried — I really tried God. I loved him dearly and I tried to help him, but he wasn't ready to accept help. I wanted so badly for this to work out because I knew he was such a good husband and father and I knew he loved us dearly. But I had to do what was best for the kids and I and after he took Leo, I didn't want to chance anything. I know I was supposed to stay married until death, but I couldn't do it. I am so sorry."

There was a long pause and in a gentle voice, I heard Him ask, "Did you love him?" I immediately replied, "Oh, I loved him with all of my heart and all of my soul."

And God said to me, "And the greatest of these is love."

I woke up bawling, but I felt this incredible weight taken off my shoulders. I don't know if that was really God but all I know that in that moment, that holy moment, I forgave myself.

And that, my friends, is the end of the story. Taking tragedy and turning it into holiness means that we need to allow the experience to change us, to mold us, to grow us so that we are stronger and more compassionate and able to support others on their journey. What happened to us is not the end of the world, it is only the beginning of a new chapter. And as we do with each chapter of our lives, we lift them up one by one, close to our hearts and say holy, holy, holy.

Printed in the United States
By Bookmasters